Genesis

Book 2

Paul Sutliff

Copyright © 2024 Sutliffian Press

All rights reserved.

No part of this book may be reproduced, stored in a retrieval system, or transmitted by any means, electronic, mechanical, photocopying, recording, or otherwise, without written permission from the author.

ISBN (Paperback): 979-8-9921204-1-7
ISBN (eBook): 979-8-9921204-0-0

FORWARD

This book is dedicated to those who are disciples in Christ. It was written for YOU! You are about to embark on a journey of depth in scripture reading. Each day's devotional was part of my personal study. I spent the time to not only read the scripture, but to look at commentaries, to study words and their meanings. I looked at context. Asked questions. Why? Because I believe the Word of God is so important, we have to dig into it to get as much as we can out of it.

What appears a short reading actually takes me about an hour. Prayer, reading His Word, studying the passages, making sure I don't go to fast, have done one important thing to my life. I hold each reading in my heart most of the day. Better yet, each reading serves to arm me for battle, by making scripture not only real, but places the Word in my heart so that I may give answers to those who have questions.

For those struggling with anything some call addictions, which I call binding sin, I believe a daily deep-dive into HIS Word, is the solution. You want out of the sin that binds you to return to it? Grab one of these devotionals. Dig into the Word of God, pray and meditate on what you read. I promise your life will be better. I can say this because my life blossomed as if I had no clue to the wonders of God, before I started this part of my life.

For those scared of doing anything in depth – I am a Special Education Teacher. I write to average people, not scholars. This book was meant for you. It is purposefully written simply for the intent of sharing the deepness and joy of reading God's Word.

If you are a pastor or chaplain doing a prison ministry and are looking for a discount on books. Please contact me at Berean_research@yahoo.com.

DAY #70
GENESIS 26:1-5

1 And there was a famine in the land, beside the first famine that was in the days of Abraham. And Isaac went unto Abimelech king of the Philistines unto Gerar.
2 And the LORD appeared unto him, and said, Go not down into Egypt; dwell in the land which I shall tell you of:
3 Sojourn in this land, and I will be with you, and will bless you; for unto you, and unto your seed, I will give all these countries, and I will perform the oath which I swore unto Abraham your father;
4 And I will make your seed to multiply as the stars of heaven, and will give unto your seed all these countries; and in your seed shall all the nations of the earth be blessed;
5 Because that Abraham obeyed my voice, and kept my charge, my commandments, my statutes, and my laws.

When famine strikes the land God promised, as it did to Abraham his father, what does Isaac do? He likely recalls the stories his father told of the past king Abimelech, the wells his father spoke of, and the relationship his father had had with the old king. So, he headed there first. It was closer to home. It would be all that much faster to return when the famine ended. Isaac thought of going to Egypt next, but God appeared to him and told him not to go there. This message from God seems in two parts because verse 2 states dwell in the land which I shall tell you of," and verse 3 starts, "Sojourn in the land." Isaac listened heard the call to go to Gerar, and was then blessed for his faithfulness to God.

Notice that where Isaac dwells, Gerar is the edge of the kingdom of the new king, Abimelech (melech is the Hebrew word for king). Isaac does not intend to intrude, but to stay on the edge, and appear non-threatening for he is only there because of a famine.

Dear Lord Jesus,

Sometimes you answer our prayers by granting us calmness and conviction and a place to go. Lord, you hear our prayers and plan for our needs before we even know we have that need. You go before us and watch over us as we follow in Your steps. Lord, You deserve all the glory for such love. Lord, I ask that You keep working on me, that I may be more like You.

In Jesus name, Amen.

DAY #71
GENESIS 26:6-11

6   And Isaac dwelt in Gerar:
7   And the men of the place asked *him* of his wife; and he said, She *is* my sister: for he feared to say, She *is* my wife; lest, *said he*, the men of the place should kill me for Rebekah; because she *was* fair to look upon.
8   And it came to pass, when he had been there a long time, that Abimelech king of the Philistines looked out at a

	window, and saw, and, behold, Isaac *was* sporting with Rebekah his wife.
9	And Abimelech called Isaac, and said, Behold, of a surety she *is* your wife: and how did you say, She *is* my sister? And Isaac said unto him, Because I said, Lest I die for her.
10	And Abimelech said, What *is* this you have done unto us? one of the people might lightly have lain with your wife, and you would have brought guiltiness upon us.
11	And Abimelech charged all *his* people, saying, He that touches this man or his wife shall surely be put to death.

You have to wonder after reading this passage if Abraham told his son Isaac, of his own sin, calling Sarah his mother, his sister when they were in Abimelech's territory before. The answer here has to be yes. Why did Isaac repeat this sin? Because he too like his father did not fully trust God? Abimelech the elder, was spoken to by God and learned of Abraham's deceit. Abimelech the younger, however, did not take Rebekah, yet. But discovered Isaac's deceit through catching them in a playful moment for husbands and wives.

Notice how the younger Abimelech, answers Isaac's response. His response was one of repulsion and called it a sin to sleep with another man's wife. Abimelech also gave an order of protection to Isaac and Rebekah. Isaac's response is not noted here. But he stays and prospers.

Dear Lord Jesus,

Help me to think before I speak. Help me to pray to know what to say. My words should be yours and not my own. I don't want to give in to temptation and argue when I can share your love and show You. Work on me God, so that others may see You and not me.

In Jesus name, Amen.

DAY #72
GENESIS 26:12-25

12 Then Isaac sowed in that land, and received in the same year an hundredfold: and the LORD blessed him.
13 And the man waxed great, and went forward, and grew until he became very great:
14 For he had possession of flocks, and possession of herds, and great store of servants: and the Philistines envied him.
15 For all the wells which his father's servants had dug in the days of Abraham his father, the Philistines had stopped them, and filled them with earth.
16 And Abimelech said unto Isaac, Go from us; for you are much mightier than we.
17 And Isaac departed there, and pitched his tent in the valley of Gerar, and dwelt there.
18 And Isaac dug again the wells of water, which they had dug in the days of Abraham his father; for the Philistines had stopped them after the death of Abraham: and he called their names after the names by which his father had called them.
19 And Isaac's servants dug in the valley, and found there a well of springing water.
20 And the herdmen of Gerar did strive with Isaac's herdmen, saying, The water *is* ours: and he called the name of the well Esek; because they strove with him.

21 And they dug another well, and strove for that also: and he called the name of it Sitnah.
22 And he removed from there, and dug another well; and for that they strove not: and he called the name of it Rehoboth; and he said, For now the LORD has made room for us, and we shall be fruitful in the land.
23 And he went up from there to Beersheba.
24 And the LORD appeared unto him the same night, and said, I *am* the God of Abraham your father: fear not, for I *am* with you, and will bless you, and multiply your seed for my servant Abraham's sake.
25 And he built an altar there, and called upon the name of the LORD, and pitched his tent there: and there Isaac's servants dug a well.

Isaac did as God asked, and dwelt in the land, and was blessed. He went from leading a troop of men and women to leading a GREAT people. His blessing was so great it enabled his men to find water and feed his flocks. Where he sowed one seed 100 times that came forth. Isaac was just a man who listened and talked to God. His prosperity and those with him grew also.

The flocks and herds, and the fields, grew so that no one could deny how great Isaac had become so great that those around him were filled with jealousy. Even Abimelech the king asked Isaac to move on due to his strength. Isaac easily moves away from trouble. Then the best thing happens! God visits Isaac, speaking to him promising to bless him and his children even more! But those outside Isaac's camp do not know of this blessing.

Isaac's success was due to his following God and being faithful. But those outside his group who stirred the people up against him never asked why he was so successful! This type of thing is a huge problem today. People do not ask how or what a person did to become successful. They don't go and ask: "how do I do this?" Instead, they create trouble and blame others for their own problems.

Dear Lord Jesus!

You deserve all my praise for all You have done in my life. Your blessings, your corrections, bring me closer to You. Please keep working on me. Place me near great men and women who love You so that I might learn from their example.

In Jesus name, Amen.

DAY #73
GENESIS 26:25-33

26 Then Abimelech went to him from Gerar, and Ahuzzath one of his friends, and Phichol the chief captain of his army.
27 And Isaac said unto them, Why do you come to me, seeing you hate me, and have sent me away from you?
28 And they said, We saw certainly that the LORD was with you: and we said, Let there be now an oath between us, *even* between us and you, and let us make a covenant with you;
29 That you will do us no hurt, as we have not touched you, and as we have done unto you nothing but good, and have sent you away in peace: you *are* now the blessed of the LORD.

30	And he made them a feast, and they did eat and drink.
31	And they rose up betimes in the morning, and swore one to another: and Isaac sent them away, and they departed from him in peace.
32	And it came to pass the same day, that Isaac's servants came, and told him concerning the well which they had dug, and said unto him, We have found water.
33	And he called it Shebah: therefore the name of the city *is* Beersheba unto this day.

How often have you heard of a ruler pursuing, with a chief of the army, to make peace? Isaac left and the blessings of his presence left with him! Abimelech had asked him to leave, fearing he could turn against him and take over the land. The purpose here was not to make a pact of peace but to ensure that Isaac would not return with an army if he grew even more and chose to take some revenge on those who told him to leave.

The place where they were became the city of Beersheba. This location has importance Biblically, Apologetically, and more! To begin with, Beersheba exists today! The "Wilderness of Beersheba" is the name given to where Hagar went after leaving Abraham ("Then she departed and wandered in the Wilderness of Beersheba." Genesis 21:14) This is Southern Israel, not towards the East as Islam claims. It was given to the tribe of Simeon (Joshua 19:2). Samuel stationed his sons there (I Samuel 8:2). Beersheba is noted as a southern capital during the time of King David (2 Samuel 24:2) and King Solomon (1 Kings 4:25).

Dear Lord Jesus,

You know our hearts. You know the reasoning that drives our actions. You know what troubles our souls. Lord, help us to overcome all of this foolishness to be the men and women of God You want us to be. Help us to be the ones who set the example of what love means. You loved us first! We can only be a poor copy of Your perfect example. Lord, make us into that! Use us so that others may see your love!

In Jesus name, Amen.

DAY #74
GENESIS 26:34-35

34   And Esau was forty years old when he took to wife Judith the daughter of Beeri the Hittite, and Bashemath the daughter of Elon the Hittite:
35   Which were a grief of mind unto Isaac and to Rebekah.

Take a moment and think about what would continually drive you nuts about your child's spouse. Try this as you think on that topic. She is a good cook and a good housekeeper. BUT, she serves other gods. She has idols that she worships and teaches the children that gods can be made of wood and stone. Everything you taught your son about good and evil is suddenly turned upside down because she says "no that's wrong."

When your son and this woman now the mother of your grandchildren visit and ask you to babysit, the children ask where your gods are because there are no idols and marvel that you can pray without repeating words and rituals.

Not asked yet, is why these men are waiting until they are older than forty to look for wives. Rather it was Abraham who put off the task of finding a wife for him. Esau was not so patient, when he was forty he picked his wife on his own without seeking the advice of his mother or father.

Dear Lord Jesus,

You love us more than our fathers and mothers ever could. You love us even knowing what we keep hidden, that horrifies our own selves. Lord, I can never understand how You can love me so easily. All I know is that others need to feel this love You have given to me. I thank You, God, that You keep working on me. Keep molding me and making me more like You. Lord, use me! Use me to share this love as never before!

In Jesus name, Amen.

DAY #75
GENESIS 27:1-41

1   And it came to pass, that when Isaac was old, and his eyes were dim, so that he could not see, he called Esau his eldest

son, and said unto him, My son: and he said unto him, Behold, *here am* I.

2 And he said, Behold now, I am old, I know not the day of my death:

3 Now therefore take, I pray you, your weapons, your quiver and your bow, and go out to the field, and take me *some* venison;

4 And make me savoury meat, such as I love, and bring *it* to me, that I may eat; that my soul may bless you before I die.

5 And Rebekah heard when Isaac spoke to Esau his son. And Esau went to the field to hunt *for* venison, *and* to bring *it*.

6 And Rebekah spoke unto Jacob her son, saying, Behold, I heard your father speak unto Esau your brother, saying,

7 Bring me venison, and make me savoury meat, that I may eat, and bless you before the LORD before my death.

8 Now therefore, my son, obey my voice according to that which I command you.

9 Go now to the flock, and fetch me from there two good kids of the goats; and I will make them savoury meat for your father, such as he loveth:

10 And you shall bring *it* to your father, that he may eat, and that he may bless you before his death.

11 And Jacob said to Rebekah his mother, Behold, Esau my brother *is* a hairy man, and I *am* a smooth man:

12 My father peradventure will feel me, and I shall seem to him as a deceiver; and I shall bring a curse upon me, and not a blessing.

13 And his mother said unto him, Upon me *be* your curse, my son: only obey my voice, and go fetch me *them*.

14 And he went, and fetched, and brought *them* to his mother: and his mother made savoury meat, such as his father loved.

15 And Rebekah took goodly raiment of her eldest son Esau, which *were* with her in the house, and put them upon Jacob her younger son:

16 And she put the skins of the kids of the goats upon his hands, and upon the smooth of his neck:

17 And she gave the savoury meat and the bread, which she had prepared, into the hand of her son Jacob.

18 And he came unto his father, and said, My father: and he said, Here *am* I; who *are* you, my son?

19 And Jacob said unto his father, I *am* Esau your firstborn; I have done according as you bade me: arise, I pray you, sit and eat of my venison, that your soul may bless me.

20 And Isaac said unto his son, How *is it* that you have found *it* so quickly, my son? And he said, Because the LORD your God brought *it* to me.

21 And Isaac said unto Jacob, Come near, I pray you, that I may feel you, my son, whether you *be* my very son Esau or not.

22 And Jacob went near unto Isaac his father; and he felt him, and said, The voice *is* Jacob's voice, but the hands *are* the hands of Esau.

23 And he discerned him not, because his hands were hairy, as his brother Esau's hands: so he blessed him.

24 And he said, *are* you my very son Esau? And he said, I *am*.

25 And he said, Bring *it* near to me, and I will eat of my son's venison, that my soul may bless you. And he brought *it* near to him, and he did eat: and he brought him wine, and he drank.

26 And his father Isaac said unto him, Come near now, and kiss me, my son.

27 And he came near, and kissed him: and he smelled the smell of his raiment, and blessed him, and said, See, the

smell of my son *is* as the smell of a field which the LORD has blessed:

28 Therefore God give you of the dew of heaven, and the fatness of the earth, and plenty of corn and wine:

29 Let people serve you, and nations bow down to you: be lord over your brethren, and let your mother's sons bow down to you: cursed *be* every one that curses you, and blessed *be* he that blesses you.

30 And it came to pass, as soon as Isaac had made an end of blessing Jacob, and Jacob was yet scarce gone out from the presence of Isaac his father, that Esau his brother came in from his hunting.

31 And he also had made savoury meat, and brought it unto his father, and said unto his father, Let my father arise, and eat of his son's venison, that your soul may bless me.

32 And Isaac his father said unto him, Who *are* you? And he said, I *am* your son, your firstborn Esau.

33 And Isaac trembled very exceedingly, and said, Who? where *is* he that has taken venison, and brought *it* me, and I have eaten of all before you came, and have blessed him? yea, *and* he shall be blessed.

34 And when Esau heard the words of his father, he cried with a great and exceeding bitter cry, and said unto his father, Bless me, *even* me also, O my father.

35 And he said, Your brother came with subtilty, and has taken away your blessing.

36 And he said, Is not he rightly named Jacob? for he has supplanted me these two times: he took away my birthright; and, behold, now he has taken away my blessing. And he said, Have you not reserved a blessing for me?

37 And Isaac answered and said unto Esau, Behold, I have made him your lord, and all his brethren have I given to

	him for servants; and with corn and wine have I sustained him: and what shall I do now unto you, my son?
38	And Esau said unto his father, Have you but one blessing, my father? bless me, *even* me also, O my father. And Esau lifted up his voice, and wept.
39	And Isaac his father answered and said unto him, Behold, your dwelling shall be the fatness of the earth, and of the dew of heaven from above;
40	And by your sword shall you live, and shall serve your brother; and it shall come to pass when you shall have the dominion, that you shall break his yoke from off your neck.
41	And Esau hated Jacob because of the blessing wherewith his father blessed him: and Esau said in his heart, The days of mourning for my father are at hand; then will I slay my brother Jacob.

Many people I respect as wiser and older throughout my life taught me that there was a birthright and a blessing and that these two were not the same thing. But, what if they were married together? The birthright could be sold, BUT what if the validity of the sale only came with the blessing being given to the buyer? Isaac clearly gave a blessing to Jacob, whom he clearly thought was Esau, that only the person with the birthright was entitled to receive. Is it possible the brothers never told their father what they had done? That one had sold his birthright easily for something to eat?

Since Rebekah knew, this placed Rebekah with some responsibility. It was not just that she loved Jacob more, her knowledge of the sale, made her responsible for sharing Esau was about to take back part of that birthright he sold.

Isaac's blessing to his sons cursed the other son. In the blessing he gave to Jacob, he cursed whom he thought was Jacob, but the curse fell on Esau. When he did bless Esau, he cursed Jacob again. This shows that the birthright was tied to the blessing. If Isaac knew about the sale of the birthright, he intended to go against the sale with the blessing he gave.

Sadly, Isaac could have worked to unite his two sons. They will have to do that on their own without their father's blessing encouraging them.

Keep in mind here that Esau and Jacob are older. They are not kids. Some Bible scholars place them in their seventies at this time! They fully would have understood the birthright and blessing and not been some naïve teenagers.

Dear Lord Jesus,

You are the King of Glory! To You all praise is due. We stupid, stubborn humans so often refuse to accept the things You have set for us to do. You give us directions or instructions and we do everything we can to fight against them like toddlers throwing tantrums. Lord, help me to be more like You! Help me Lord, to fight my own will and desires. Replace them with Your own!

In Jesus name, Amen.

DAY #76
GENESIS 27:41-28:7

41 And Esau hated Jacob because of the blessing wherewith his father blessed him: and Esau said in his heart, The days of mourning for my father are at hand; then will I slay my brother Jacob.

42 And these words of Esau her elder son were told to Rebekah: and she sent and called Jacob her younger son, and said unto him, Behold, your brother Esau, as touching you, does comfort himself, *purposing* to kill you.

43 Now therefore, my son, obey my voice; and arise, flee you to Laban my brother to Haran;

44 And tarry with him a few days, until your brother's fury turn away;

45 Until your brother's anger turn away from you, and he forgets *that* which you have done to him: then I will send, and fetch you from there: why should I be deprived also of you both in one day?

46 And Rebekah said to Isaac, I am weary of my life because of the daughters of Heth: if Jacob take a wife of the daughters of Heth, such as these *which are* of the daughters of the land, what good shall my life do me?

28:1 And Isaac called Jacob, and blessed him, and charged him, and said unto him, You shall not take a wife of the daughters of Canaan.

2 Arise, go to Padanaram, to the house of Bethuel your mother's father; and take you a wife from there of the daughters of Laban your mother's brother.

3 And God Almighty bless you, and make you fruitful, and multiply you, that you may be a multitude of people;

4	And give you the blessing of Abraham, to you, and to your seed with you; that you may inherit the land wherein you are a stranger, which God gave unto Abraham.
5	And Isaac sent away Jacob: and he went to Padanaram unto Laban, son of Bethuel the Syrian, the brother of Rebekah, Jacob's and Esau's mother.
6	When Esau saw that Isaac had blessed Jacob, and sent him away to Padanaram, to take him a wife from there; and that as he blessed him he gave him a charge, saying, You shall not take a wife of the daughters of Canaan;
7	And that Jacob obeyed his father and his mother, and was gone to Padanaram;

Rachel hears of the murderous hatred of Esau and sees God's hand is this for her and Isaac to do what they should have already! Esau married at forty! It is estimated that Jacob still had no wife at the age of seventy by some Bible scholars! The stealing of the blessing by Jacob was not by a teenager. It was by a seventy-something old man! Thus, Isaac recognizes the wisdom his wife brings to him. When it was time to find wives for their twins, they should have looked to cousins, since they seemed to know who God was! They had the same set of morals. Rebekah was having a hard time with Esau's wives. They were NOT godly, and they did things that drove Rebekah to anger and disappointment. THIS TIME with the youngest (by mere seconds), they would get it right! They sent Jacob to find a wife.

The way this is worded though it appears that Rebekah planted the idea of going to his uncle Laban because of his brother's anger first. Note that she omitted obtaining a wife until she spoke with her husband, the head of the family. This was something that should be heard from Jacob's father.

Even Esau notes the directions given to Jacob and thinks about it, considering he had done the opposite. These words were said to the servant of Abraham when he was sent out to find a wife for Isaac. Without a doubt, they were told to him many times. In an oral tradition community, that story should have been retold many times to the boys as they grew.

Verse 7 says, "Jacob obeyed his father and mother." Rebekah was getting two things by sending her son away, Jacob's safety, and what she believed would be a good daughter-in-law!

Dear Lord Jesus,

Some of us can plan ahead, while many of us live in the moment. Lord, be my planner! You see farther ahead than I can imagine. You know what it is to come, and what I need to do to accomplish Your desires for my life. Lord, please focus my life and energy on the things that will bring YOU glory. Lord, bless my children.

In Jesus name, Amen.

DAY #77
GENESIS 28:8-9

8   And Esau seeing that the daughters of Canaan pleased not Isaac his father;
9   Then went Esau unto Ishmael, and took unto the wives which he had Mahalath the daughter of Ishmael Abraham's son, the sister of Nebajoth, to be his wife.

Here is the evidence that Esau was clueless. He did not understand why the daughters of Canaan did not please his mother or father. Worse, He didn't seem to care that his wives aggravated his mother, but when he learned they bothered his father, he went and took more wives! But, this time he went to Isaac's brother, Ishmael. This is problematic on a whole other level. Ishmael was the son Abraham was willing to accept, but NOT the son of promise. Ishmael and his mother Hagar, were removed from their community. It's one thing to choose a wife with a family that has no problem with idolatry. But going to another side of his family, that accepts other gods? How is that different? Ishmael's mother found a wife for him in Egypt. This was a land of other gods.

Jacob was sent to Laban because the father of Rebehah and Laban (Nahor) had the same God as Isaac's father! Sadly, these choices of Esau prove why he was not to lead the family. They prove why he was rejected by God for his younger brother.

Even the New Testament tells Christians not to marry unbelievers. "Be you not unequally yoked together with unbelievers: for what fellowship has righteousness with unrighteousness? and what communion has light with darkness? (II Corinthians 6:14).

Dear Lord Jesus,

Thank you for this lesson on the cluelessness of Esau. I want to be the person who truly understands before I act rashly. Lord, help me to not only listen but to understand. Lord, work on me. Make my ears open, my mouth quitter and my questions pointed so that I may become blessed by Your wisdom.

In Jesus name, Amen.

DAY #78
GENESIS 28:10-22

10   And Jacob went out from Beersheba, and went toward Haran.
11   And he lighted upon a certain place, and tarried there all night, because the sun was set; and he took of the stones of that place, and put *them for* his pillows, and lay down in that place to sleep.
12   And he dreamed, and behold a ladder set up on the earth, and the top of it reached to heaven: and behold the angels of God ascending and descending on it.
13   And, behold, the LORD stood above it, and said, I *am* the LORD God of Abraham your father, and the God of Isaac: the land whereon you lay, to you will I give it, and to your seed;
14   And your seed shall be as the dust of the earth, and you shall spread abroad to the west, and to the east, and to the north, and to the south: and in you and in your seed shall all the families of the earth be blessed.
15   And, behold, I *am* with you, and will keep you in all *places* where you go, and will bring you again into this land; for I will not leave you, until I have done *that* which I have spoken to you of.
16   And Jacob awakened out of his sleep, and he said, Surely the LORD is in this place; and I knew *it* not.
17   And he was afraid, and said, How dreadful *is* this place! this *is* none other but the house of God, and this *is* the gate of heaven.

18   And Jacob rose up early in the morning, and took the stone that he had put *for* his pillows, and set it up *for* a pillar, and poured oil upon the top of it.

19   And he called the name of that place Bethel: but the name of that city *was called* Luz at the first.

20   And Jacob vowed a vow, saying, If God will be with me, and will keep me in this way that I go, and will give me bread to eat, and raiment to put on,

21   So that I come again to my father's house in peace; then shall the LORD be my God:

22   And this stone, which I have set *for* a pillar, shall be God's house: and of all that you shall give me I will surely give the tenth unto you.

Dreams are usually of something we know about. They review or fantasize about things we know about. Jacob had a dream that went beyond this. He was asleep, but what he saw was beyond his memories and understanding. A ladder with angels going both up and down. Angel is the word for messenger. It doesn't mean they had wings. They used that ladder. It is also possible that ladder was the only word that Jacob could think of to describe what he saw. But what he saw was not as important as what he heard.

The words were stronger than the blessing his father Isaac gave to him. One was well wishes, this was promised! These words were not said to a teen or a twenty-something. Jacob was in his young seventies these words had great meaning.

Bethel literally means the House of God. The act of memorializing memories of places where man encounters God is something we should still do today. Imagine the things we could learn if we all did this. There are a few such places in my life, that cause me to think about those encounters when I pass by. The thing that seems undeniable to me when I do pass by those spots is that God met me there!

But perhaps the most powerful thing here is a new mention of the tithe. We heard about it first when Abraham gave a tenth to Melchizedek in Genesis 14. Now Jacob promises a tithe. This is something we practice today as believers in Christ. Giving a tenth of our income. To some, this sounds like a lot. But the reality is that while we attempt to bless God with this. He returns the blessing far more than we can comprehend.

Dear Lord Jesus,

How is it that you call on us, and we do not listen? How many times have you called on us and we try to silence Your still small voice by doing the opposite. Lord Jesus, don't just open my ears, cause me to act. Do not let me stand by and watch sadness unfold. Use me, Lord, make me into the person You want me to be so that others may know of Your love.

In Jesus name, Amen.

DAY #79
GENESIS 29:1-12

1   Then Jacob went on his journey, and came into the land of the people of the east.
2   And he looked, and behold a well in the field, and, lo, there *were* three flocks of sheep lying by it; for out of that well

	they watered the flocks: and a great stone *was* upon the well's mouth.
3	And thither were all the flocks gathered: and they rolled the stone from the well's mouth, and watered the sheep, and put the stone again upon the well's mouth in his place.
4	And Jacob said unto them, My brethren, whence *be* you? And they said, Of Haran *are* we.
5	And he said unto them, Know you Laban the son of Nahor? And they said, We know *him*.
6	And he said unto them, *is* he well? And they said, *He is* well: and, behold, Rachel his daughter comes with the sheep.
7	And he said, Lo, *it is* yet high day, neither *is it* time that the cattle should be gathered together: water you the sheep, and go *and* feed *them*.
8	And they said, We cannot, until all the flocks be gathered together, and *till* they roll the stone from the well's mouth; then we water the sheep.
9	And while he yet spoke with them, Rachel came with her father's sheep: for she kept them.
10	And it came to pass, when Jacob saw Rachel the daughter of Laban his mother's brother, and the sheep of Laban his mother's brother, that Jacob went near, and rolled the stone from the well's mouth, and watered the flock of Laban his mother's brother.
11	And Jacob kissed Rachel, and lifted up his voice, and wept.
12	And Jacob told Rachel that he *was* her father's brother, and that he *was* Rebekah's son: and she ran and told her father.

Jacob has always been a bit different. He is the child who took after his mother. He was not what some may call a "manly man" til this point. Before he set off, he must have heard about the story of how his mother came to be his father's wife. He must have heard how the servant went to the well, after seeking God, and how quickly God granted his requests.

Jacob is a man who watches and observes. He watches the sheep, their shepherds and talks to them. He watched them easily water their flock by moving a stone of considerable size, something he did not expect a girl capable of doing. He asked the shepherds to help her. They refused. As a result, the observer becomes a man of action. He goes and moves the stone AND waters her flock. Jacob had to be thinking about who she was, not just her beauty. Rachel was a potential wife. But he came with nothing to give for her dowry. This is somewhat unusual, considering Abraham sent his servant with gifts for Isaac's future wife. This may be a statement of Isaac's punishment because Jacob tricked him to obtain Esau's blessing.

"Jacob lifted up his voice and wept." There are three other uses of "lifted up and wept, that can be found in Judges 9:7, 21:2, and II Samuel 13:36. When reading this it is important to understand that this means Jacob gave thanks and praise to God for having found Rachel. However, Jacob took the liberty of kissing Rachel first. This shows that Jacob does not always get his priorities straight. He praises God second. This speaks of lessons to come for Jacob.

Dear Lord Jesus,

You do so much for our lives that we can never grasp how much love you express to each and every moment. Lord, help us to get our priorities straight. You should be first in our lives. Help us to get that right, so we can better share with others this endless love

You have for us! Embolden us to share that love even today with someone who needs to hear of this love You have for us sinners.

In Jesus name, Amen.

DAY #80
GENESIS 29:13-30

13 And it came to pass, when Laban heard the tidings of Jacob his sister's son, that he ran to meet him, and embraced him, and kissed him, and brought him to his house. And he told Laban all these things.
14 And Laban said to him, Surely you *are* my bone and my flesh. And he abode with him the space of a month.
15 And Laban said unto Jacob, Because you *are* my brother, should you therefore serve me for nought? tell me, what *shall* your wages *be*?
16 And Laban had two daughters: the name of the elder *was* Leah, and the name of the younger *was* Rachel.
17 Leah *was* tender eyed; but Rachel was beautiful and well favoured.
18 And Jacob loved Rachel; and said, I will serve you seven years for Rachel your younger daughter.
19 And Laban said, *it is* better that I give her to you, than that I should give her to another man: abide with me.
20 And Jacob served seven years for Rachel; and they seemed unto him *but* a few days, for the love he had to her.
21 And Jacob said unto Laban, Give *me* my wife, for my days are fulfilled, that I may go in unto her.

22	And Laban gathered together all the men of the place, and made a feast.
23	And it came to pass in the evening, that he took Leah his daughter, and brought her to him; and he went in unto her.
24	And Laban gave unto his daughter Leah Zilpah his maid *for* an handmaid.
25	And it came to pass, that in the morning, behold, it *was* Leah: and he said to Laban, What *is* this you have done unto me? did not I serve with you for Rachel? why then have you beguiled me?
26	And Laban said, It must not be so done in our country, to give the younger before the firstborn.
27	Fulfil her week, and we will give you this also for the service which you shall serve with me yet seven other years.
28	And Jacob did so, and fulfilled her week: and he gave him Rachel his daughter to wife also.
29	And Laban gave to Rachel his daughter Bilhah his handmaid to be her maid.
30	And he went in also unto Rachel, and he loved also Rachel more than Leah, and served with him yet seven other years.

It is said that love is blind. Jacob offered seven years of labor for the woman he loved. Think about the current job you or someone you know has, and the amount paid involved times seven. Working those seven years not for money, but for the payment of a spouse at the end. This was what Jacob agreed to since he brought no dowry with him. Jacob must truly have thought Rachel was of great value to agree to invest seven years of his life for her.

The wedding ceremony is the consummation act in a tent. Jacob somehow has no clue who he made love to until the next morning. The answers to how this is possible are many, but the obvious is probably correct. Jacob had too much to drink when he entered that tent. Jacob, the man who tricked his own father, becomes the one who is tricked. At the least, he was tricked into this by just his Uncle Laban and Leah. At the worst, Rachel was also involved in this act of deceit. No details are revealed here.

Laban makes the excuse that culture and tradition forced him to do this. Then he easily gets seven more years of free labor from Jacob to give him, his beloved Rachel. In all, Jacob worked fourteen years to marry Rachel.

Jacob now finds himself with two wives. One was worth seven years of his life, the other worth fourteen years. Is it any surprise he valued one over the other?

Think about this. When Jacob started this arrangement he was in his young seventies. When he finished fourteen years of labor, he was well into his nineties! These sound like the arrangements of a teenager, not that of a man in his forties. He had invested seven years of his life into a relationship with Rachel, and would not leave without her after seven years. He could have.

Dear Lord Jesus,

Be the force behind all that I do. Be the reason, the real purpose of my love, my work, my passion, even my interactions with those I meet in passing. Lord, do not let me be easily duped through my own foolishness. Push me onward to strive for excellence in all that I do, so that YOU may be magnified. Not myself. Please work on me. Change me from within. Refine me into someone others are able to see You more than my own self.

In Jesus name, Amen.

DAY #81
GENESIS 29:31-35

31   And when the LORD saw that Leah *was* hated, he opened her womb: but Rachel *was* barren.
32   And Leah conceived, and bare a son, and she called his name Reuben: for she said, Surely the LORD has looked upon my affliction; now therefore my husband will love me.
33   And she conceived again, and bare a son; and said, Because the LORD has heard that I *was* hated, he has therefore given me this *son* also: and she called his name Simeon.
34   And she conceived again, and bare a son; and said, Now this time will my husband be joined unto me, because I have born him three sons: therefore was his name called Levi.
35   And she conceived again, and bare a son: and she said, Now will I praise the LORD: therefore she called his name Judah; and left bearing.

Jacob now has two wives and treats one poorly while still madly in love with Rachel. But, in this, he still is intimate with Leah regularly enough that she is able to be blessed with children.

Leah proves to be an example of why Jacob's mother, Rebekah wanted him to find a wife from her brother's children. Leah knows God! She loves him! She also wants the love of her husband, but that is secondary. How great is the Lord, who opens wombs is expressed by her naming of her children. Reuben – "for the Lord has looked upon my affliction." Simeon – "the Lord has heard." Levi – "joined," for her hopes of her husband being joined to her. The fourth child, Judah – "PRAISE!" Jacob may have loved Rachel, but here we do something special! Here we have the father of the tribe, from which Luke 3:33 bears witness that Jesus' heritage demonstrates. Jesus comes from the tribe "PRAISE!" Jesus is the Lion of the tribe of Judah" (Genesis 49:9).

Leah leaves childbearing here. She has honored God and sought the love of her husband.

Dear Lord Jesus,

Help me to honor You with the gifts You give to me. I am lazy, foolish, and deserve nothing but Your wrath. Yet, You gave me gifts. Lord, may I use them to bring you glory. Lord, may my children also be those gifts that bring You honor and praise, such that their children's children call on You with such love that they too will never wonder at who You are.

In Jesus name, Amen.

DAY #82
GENESIS 30:1-24

1   And when Rachel saw that she bare Jacob no children, Rachel envied her sister; and said unto Jacob, Give me children, or else I die.
2   And Jacob's anger was kindled against Rachel: and he said, *am* I in God's stead, who has withheld from you the fruit of the womb?

3   And she said, Behold my maid Bilhah, go in unto her; and she shall bear upon my knees, that I may also have children by her.
4   And she gave him Bilhah her handmaid to wife: and Jacob went in unto her.
5   And Bilhah conceived, and bare Jacob a son.
6   And Rachel said, God has judged me, and has also heard my voice, and has given me a son: therefore called she his name Dan.
7   And Bilhah Rachel's maid conceived again, and bare Jacob a second son.
8   And Rachel said, With great wrestlings have I wrestled with my sister, and I have prevailed: and she called his name Naphtali.
9   When Leah saw that she had left bearing, she took Zilpah her maid, and gave her Jacob to wife.
10   And Zilpah Leah's maid bare Jacob a son.
11   And Leah said, A troop comes: and she called his name Gad.
12   And Zilpah Leah's maid bare Jacob a second son.
13   And Leah said, Happy am I, for the daughters will call me blessed: and she called his name Asher.
14   And Reuben went in the days of wheat harvest, and found mandrakes in the field, and brought them unto his mother Leah. Then Rachel said to Leah, Give me, I pray you, of your son's mandrakes.
15   And she said unto her, *is it* a small matter that you have taken my husband? and would you take away my son's mandrakes also? And Rachel said, Therefore he shall lie with you tonight for your son's mandrakes.
16   And Jacob came out of the field in the evening, and Leah went out to meet him, and said, You must come in unto me; for surely I have hired you with my son's mandrakes. And he lay with her that night.

17	And God listened unto Leah, and she conceived, and bare Jacob the fifth son.
18	And Leah said, God has given me my hire, because I have given my maiden to my husband: and she called his name Issachar.
19	And Leah conceived again, and bare Jacob the sixth son.
20	And Leah said, God has endued me [with] a good dowry; now will my husband dwell with me, because I have born him six sons: and she called his name Zebulun.
21	And afterwards she bare a daughter, and called her name Dinah.
22	And God remembered Rachel, and God listened to her, and opened her womb.
23	And she conceived, and bare a son; and said, God has taken away my reproach:
24	And she called his name Joseph; and said, The LORD shall add to me another son.

Most kids with brothers and sisters have some sibling rivalry. One always wants to be the best at this or that. The fastest! The first! Just like in life, no one wants to be last in a race, nor wants to be told you might as well give up. The I and me, between Leah and Rachel, display their competitiveness and their inability to just get along with each other.

The mandrake story is an oddity, but it shows that Rachel would sell her night with Jacob for a plant. Smith's Bible Dictionary states that Mandrakes are thought to be a plant that has the "power to excite voluptuousness." It has the properties of a stimulant. The Arabs call it the "devil's apple."

Dear Lord Jesus,

Sometimes we wander in our attempts to follow you. We do not walk that straight path. Instead, we find distractions easily and walk away from the task you assigned us to complete. Lord, strengthen our resolve to do what you have given us to do.

In Jesus name, Amen.

DAY #83
GENESIS 30:25-43

25 And it came to pass, when Rachel had born Joseph, that Jacob said unto Laban, Send me away, that I may go unto mine own place, and to my country.
26 Give *me* my wives and my children, for whom I have served you, and let me go: for you know my service which I have done you.
27 And Laban said unto him, I pray you, if I have found favour in your eyes, *tarry: for* I have learned by experience that the LORD has blessed me for your sake.
28 And he said, Appoint me your wages, and I will give *it*.
29 And he said unto him, You know how I have served you, and how your cattle was with me.
30 For *it was* little which you had before I *came*, and it is *now* increased unto a multitude; and the LORD has blessed you since my coming: and now when shall I provide for mine own house also?

31 And he said, What shall I give you? And Jacob said, You shall not give me any thing: if you will do this thing for me, I will again feed *and* keep your flock:

32 I will pass through all your flock to day, removing from there all the speckled and spotted cattle, and all the brown cattle among the sheep, and the spotted and speckled among the goats: and *of such* shall be my hire.

33 So shall my righteousness answer for me in time to come, when it shall come for my hire before your face: every one that *is* not speckled and spotted among the goats, and brown among the sheep, that shall be counted stolen with me.

34 And Laban said, Behold, I would it might be according to your word.

35 And he removed that day the he goats that were ringstraked and spotted, and all the she goats that were speckled and spotted, *and* every one that had *some* white in it, and all the brown among the sheep, and gave *them* into the hand of his sons.

36 And he set three days' journey between himself and Jacob: and Jacob fed the rest of Laban's flocks.

37 And Jacob took him rods of green poplar, and of the hazel and chesnut tree; and pilled white strakes in them, and made the white appear which *was* in the rods.

38 And he set the rods which he had pilled before the flocks in the gutters in the watering troughs when the flocks came to drink, that they should conceive when they came to drink.

39 And the flocks conceived before the rods, and brought forth cattle ringstraked, speckled, and spotted.

40 And Jacob did separate the lambs, and set the faces of the flocks toward the ringstraked, and all the brown in the flock of Laban; and he put his own flocks by themselves, and put them not unto Laban's cattle.

41 And it came to pass, whensoever the stronger cattle did conceive, that Jacob laid the rods before the eyes of the cattle in the gutters, that they might conceive among the rods.

42 But when the cattle were feeble, he put *them* not in: so the feebler were Laban's, and the stronger Jacob's.

43 And the man increased exceedingly, and had much cattle, and maidservants, and menservants, and camels, and asses.

It was time for Jacob to go home. Laban acknowledged this and told Jacob to decide what his wages should be. In today's world, you would never see a boss asking what you want for your work and simply accepting an answer he was given. This says two things about Jacob's character. That he was both honest and fair. He had not given Laban a reason to distrust him. We also find here that Laban openly admits his possessions became great after Jacob came to work to earn his wives. Laban's greed and his way of weaving words again show him as attempting to deceive Jacob to stay on as his main shepherd.

Jacob sets his wages and sets about to feed the flock a last time. This time seems defined and is probably at the least season. During this time his chosen wages make him great in wealth. Even though he chose as his wages, the lesser valued sheep, his own become the stronger. Note that Laban's sheep do not seem cared for, but Laban has sons who should be caring for the flock also.

Dear Lord Jesus,

You work on us from within, you take a liar, and change his heart set on deception into a man set to share the Truth. You do the impossible! Lord, may my wages bring prosperity in this world, but more so store up treasures in heaven. Embolden me to share Your word.

In Jesus name, Amen.

DAY #84
GENESIS 31:1-18

1 And he heard the words of Laban's sons, saying, Jacob has taken away all that *was* our father's; and of *that* which *was* our father's has he gotten all this glory.
2 And Jacob beheld the countenance of Laban, and, behold, it *was* not toward him as before.
3 And the LORD said unto Jacob, Return unto the land of your fathers, and to your kindred; and I will be with you.
4 And Jacob sent and called Rachel and Leah to the field unto his flock,
5 And said unto them, I see your father's countenance, that it *is* not toward me as before; but the God of my father has been with me.
6 And you know that with all my power I have served your father.
7 And your father has deceived me, and changed my wages ten times; but God does not allow him to hurt me.
8 If he said thus, The speckled shall be your wages; then all the cattle bare speckled: and if he said thus, The ringstraked shall be your hire; then bare all the cattle ringstraked.
9 Thus God has taken away the cattle of your father, and given *them* to me.

10   And it came to pass at the time that the cattle conceived, that I lifted up mine eyes, and saw in a dream, and, behold, the rams which leaped upon the cattle *were* ringstraked, speckled, and grisled.
11   And the angel of God spoke unto me in a dream, *saying*, Jacob: And I said, Here *am* I.
12   And he said, Lift up now your eyes, and see, all the rams which leap upon the cattle *are* ringstraked, speckled, and grisled: for I have seen all that Laban doeth unto you.
13   I *am* the God of Bethel, where you anointed the pillar, *and* where you vowed a vow unto me: now arise, get you out from this land, and return unto the land of your kindred.
14   And Rachel and Leah answered and said unto him, *Is there* yet any portion or inheritance for us in our father's house?
15   Are we not counted of him strangers? for he has sold us, and has quite devoured also our money.
16   For all the riches which God has taken from our father, that *is* ours, and our children's: now then, whatsoever God has said unto you, do.
17   Then Jacob rose up, and set his sons and his wives upon camels;
18   And he carried away all his cattle, and all his goods which he had gotten, the cattle of his getting, which he had gotten in Padanaram, for to go to Isaac his father in the land of Canaan.

Jacob is tired of dealing with Laban's greed. He was the one who originally said, "set your wages." Jacob worked hard caring for the flocks while he was there. God rewarded him with blessings no matter what the change in wages was. Now, God tells Jacob to go home to the land of his fathers. Jacob must leave now. He can no longer tarry. Regardless of what Laban wants, this time Jacob has to leave. As a good husband, he discusses these things with his wives. Here we see how the characteristic of greed was passed from Laban, not only to his sons but to his daughters as well. Yes, they are right, that they were sold, but the feeling of entitlement to inheritance before their father was dead, was pure greed. This says nothing to the fact that because they were daughters, the inheritance would be split by the brothers not them.

Dear Lord Jesus,

Thank You for giving direction to my life as You did for Jacob. You intervene, protect, and even provide guidance. You watch over every little thing to help me make each step. Lord, help me to return this love You have by being more like You each day.

In Jesus name, Amen.

DAY #85
GENESIS 31:19-55

19   And Laban went to shear his sheep: and Rachel had stolen the images that *were* her father's.
20   And Jacob stole away unawares to Laban the Syrian, in that he told him not that he fled.
21   So he fled with all that he had; and he rose up, and passed over the river, and set his face *toward* the mount Gilead.
22   And it was told Laban on the third day that Jacob was fled.

23   And he took his brethren with him, and pursued after him seven days' journey; and they overtook him in the mount Gilead.

24   And God came to Laban the Syrian in a dream by night, and said unto him, Take heed that you speak not to Jacob either good or bad.

25   Then Laban overtook Jacob. Now Jacob had pitched his tent in the mount: and Laban with his brethren pitched in the mount of Gilead.

26   And Laban said to Jacob, What have you done, that you have stolen away unawares to me, and carried away my daughters, as captives *taken* with the sword?

27   Why did you flee away secretly, and steal away from me; and did not tell me, that I might have sent you away with mirth, and with songs, with tabret, and with harp?

28   And have not allowed me to kiss my sons and my daughters? you have now done foolishly in *so* doing.

29   It is in the power of my hand to do you hurt: but the God of your father spoke unto me last night, saying, Take you heed that you speak not to Jacob either good or bad.

30   And now, *though* you would needs be gone, because you sore long after your father's house, *yet* why have you stolen my gods?

31   And Jacob answered and said to Laban, Because I was afraid: for I said, Peradventure you would take by force your daughters from me.

32   With whomsoever you find your gods, let him not live: before our brethren discern you what *is* your with me, and take *it* to you. For Jacob knew not that Rachel had stolen them.

33   And Laban went into Jacob's tent, and into Leah's tent, and into the two maidservants' tents; but he found *them*

not. Then went he out of Leah's tent, and entered into Rachel's tent.

34 Now Rachel had taken the images, and put them in the camel's furniture, and sat upon them. And Laban searched all the tent, but found *them* not.

35 And she said to her father, Let it not displease my lord that I cannot rise up before you; for the custom of women *is* upon me. And he searched, but found not the images.

36 And Jacob was very angry, and chode with Laban: and Jacob answered and said to Laban, What *is* my trespass? what *is* my sin, that you have so hotly pursued after me?

37 Whereas you have searched all my stuff, what have you found of all your household stuff? set *it* here before my brethren and your brethren, that they may judge between us both.

38 This twenty years *have* I *been* with you; your ewes and your she goats have not cast their young, and the rams of your flock have I not eaten.

39 That which was torn *of beasts* I brought not unto you; I bare the loss of it; of my hand did you require it, *whether* stolen by day, or stolen by night.

40 *Thus* I was; in the day the drought consumed me, and the frost by night; and my sleep departed from mine eyes.

41 Thus have I been twenty years in your house; I served you fourteen years for your two daughters, and six years for your cattle: and you have changed my wages ten times.

42 Except the God of my father, the God of Abraham, and the fear of Isaac, had been with me, surely you had sent me away now empty. God has seen mine affliction and the labour of my hands, and rebuked *you* last night.

43 And Laban answered and said unto Jacob, *These* daughters *are* my daughters, and *these* children *are* my children, and *these* cattle *are* my cattle, and all that you see *is* mine: and

what can I do this day unto these my daughters, or unto their children which they have born?

44 Now therefore come you, let us make a covenant, I and you; and let it be for a witness between me and you.

45 And Jacob took a stone, and set it up *for* a pillar.

46 And Jacob said unto his brethren, Gather stones; and they took stones, and made an heap: and they did eat there upon the heap.

47 And Laban called it Jegarsahadutha: but Jacob called it Galeed.

48 And Laban said, This heap *is* a witness between me and you this day. Therefore was the name of it called Galeed;

49 And Mizpah; for he said, The LORD watch between me and you, when we are absent one from another.

50 If you shall afflict my daughters, or if you shall take *other* wives beside my daughters, no man *is* with us; see, God *is* witness between me and you.

51 And Laban said to Jacob, Behold this heap, and behold *this* pillar, which I have cast between me and you;

52 This heap *be* witness, and *this* pillar *be* witness, that I will not pass over this heap to you, and that you shall not pass over this heap and this pillar unto me, for harm.

53 The God of Abraham, and the God of Nahor, the God of their father, judge between us. And Jacob swore by the fear of his father Isaac.

54 Then Jacob offered sacrifice upon the mount, and called his brethren to eat bread: and they did eat bread, and tarried all night in the mount.

55 And early in the morning Laban rose up, and kissed his sons and his daughters, and blessed them: and Laban departed, and returned unto his place.

Laban's greed and foolishness in serving other gods have overtaken his ability to reason. If a god could be stolen, was it worthy of worship? NO! Laban knew Jacob did not serve idols. He had to have a clue that it was one of his own children who took the idols. Laban claims they stole away and says nothing about the changes of wages, except that all Jacob has once belonged to him, and when they are almost done speaking, Laban again says all that Jacob has is his. Such greed. Such utter foolishness! Serving fake gods steals a man's reason as much as greed changes people into uncaring selfish individuals.

Jacob had no reason to believe someone with him stole anything, much less his wife Rachel, who owes God a huge thank you for not having Jacob or Laban making her move and revealing her crime. But the reason for the pursuit was not the loss of idols. It was the loss of all that Jacob had. Laban had always considered his daughters, son-in-law, and flocks all his and his alone. Discovering they had left, hit Laban with the reality that his children had grown up, and had married had children, and went with their husband. The very man who earned what he had from Laban, and now all that was gone. He was left with two lazy sons, who could never bring his prosperity back to how Jacob's presence was blessed by God.

Dear Lord Jesus,

I can never grasp how it is that You love me so much and bless me even though I am truly unworthy of such wonders. Lord, please continue to work on me. Please change my heart even more so that others may see You before they see me. You deserve the glory for the work and changes You have created in me.

In Jesus name, Amen.

DAY #86
GENESIS 32:1-2

1   And Jacob went on his way, and the angels of God met him.
2   And when Jacob saw them, he said, This *is* God's host: and he called the name of that place Mahanaim.

Jacob has done what God asked. He returns to Canaan. There God send his messengers the angels to meet him. These angels are not flying around like fairies. They are seen as messengers of God! They appear as men.

Just as when a person accepts Christ, and there is a celebration in heaven for that person's salvation, the angels this day are here to celebrate the return of the first prodigal son. Jacob was called, he answered. Not only he came but he returned with everything he had. He did not return alone to test if it was safe. He did not come without fear over what he had done that led to his leaving. But he came still with all that he had. This is wholehearted devotion.

Jacob left a cunning and deceitful man. How has he returned? He was in his 70s when he left. Now he is around 90. Has Jacob changed? He has been on the other side of deceit. He just confronted that deceiver (Laban). Did he threaten death as his brother did to him? Think about the changes here. Jacob worshipped God with that deceiver and embraced him before he departed. By the time he gets to where the angels greet him, Jacob has a whole other mindset.

He celebrates the presence of the angels by naming the place Mahanaim.

Dear Lord Jesus,

Guide my steps. I am one who easily forgets where my feet should go. Lord, give me a greater desire to dive deep into Your Word. I want to be more like You. I want my life to reflect Your love. Not my own foolishness. Lord, strengthen me and at the same time humble me. Remove from me pride for simply doing what You ask of me. I am Yours. Lord, direct my path.

In Jesus name, Amen.

DAY #87
GENESIS 32:3-23

3   And Jacob sent messengers before him to Esau his brother unto the land of Seir, the country of Edom.
4   And he commanded them, saying, Thus shall you speak unto my lord Esau; Your servant Jacob says thus, I have sojourned with Laban, and stayed there until now:
5   And I have oxen, and asses, flocks, and men-servants, and women-servants: and I have sent to tell my lord, that I may find grace in your sight.
6   And the messengers returned to Jacob, saying, We came to your brother Esau, and also he comes to meet you, and four hundred men with him.
7   Then Jacob was greatly afraid and distressed: and he divided the people that *was* with him, and the flocks, and herds, and the camels, into two bands;

8 And said, If Esau come to the one company, and smite it, then the other company which is left shall escape.
9 And Jacob said, O God of my father Abraham, and God of my father Isaac, the LORD which said unto me, Return unto your country, and to your kindred, and I will deal well with you:
10 I am not worthy of the least of all the mercies, and of all the truth, which you have shown unto your servant; for with my staff I passed over this Jordan; and now I am become two bands.
11 Deliver me, I pray you, from the hand of my brother, from the hand of Esau: for I fear him, lest he will come and smite me, *and* the mother with the children.
12 And you said, I will surely do you good, and make your seed as the sand of the sea, which cannot be numbered for multitude.
13 And he lodged there that same night; and took of that which came to his hand a present for Esau his brother;
14 Two hundred she goats, and twenty he goats, two hundred ewes, and twenty rams,
15 Thirty milch camels with their colts, forty cows, and ten bulls, twenty she asses, and ten foals.
16 And he delivered *them* into the hand of his servants, every drove by themselves; and said unto his servants, Pass over before me, and put a space between drove and drove.
17 And he commanded the foremost, saying, When Esau my brother meets you, and asks you, saying, Whose *are* you? and where goes you? and whose *are* these before you?
18 Then you shall say, *They be* your servant Jacob's; it *is* a present sent unto my lord Esau: and, behold, also he *is* behind us.

19   And so commanded he the second, and the third, and all that followed the droves, saying, On this manner shall you speak unto Esau, when you find him.

20   And say you moreover, Behold, your servant Jacob *is* behind us. For he said, I will appease him with the present that goes before me, and afterward I will see his face; peradventure he will accept of me.

21   So went the present over before him: and himself lodged that night in the company.

22   And he rose up that night, and took his two wives, and his two women-servants, and his eleven sons, and passed over the ford Jabbok.

23   And he took them, and sent them over the brook, and sent over that he had.

Jacob now understands the anger resulting from having been deceived not once but multiple times. He held that wrath in his hand and chose not to act. But his twin brother was always a man of action. He enjoyed the hunt. Jacob, saw himself now as prey that was coming to meet its hunter. He had "tested the water," by sending forth gifts. Now Esau and 400 men came in "hot pursuit." Jacob felt like a fool and fear overwhelmed him, even though he had heard God say go home. He pleads with God but takes care to protect his family at the risk of his own life. Isn't this what a husband is supposed to do? Isn't he supposed to get down on his knees and seek God for his family? Isn't the husband supposed to lead? Isn't the husband the one responsible for protecting the wife and children? That night he was to be the last line of defense before his family.

We as humans fear what is not known. Jacob feared his twin brother partly because he now truly understood the hotness of that anger. He understood deceit is not something you easily forget.

Dear Lord Jesus,

Strengthen me! Make me stronger in You! Help me to stand in such a way that I will not just be physically able to stand, but ready to combat the evil in this world by being ready with Your Word to take on spiritual attacks. Let me be the one who stands in the gap for my family. Let me be the one responsible to stand in that gap. Lord, You have done all for us! How can I do less for those whom I love most?

In Jesus name, Amen.

DAY #88
GENESIS 32:24-32

24   And Jacob was left alone; and there wrestled a man with him until the breaking of the day.
25   And when he saw that he prevailed not against him, he touched the hollow of his thigh; and the hollow of Jacob's thigh was out of joint, as he wrestled with him.
26   And he said, Let me go, for the day breaks. And he said, I will not let you go, except you bless me.
27   And he said unto him, What *is* your name? And he said, Jacob.

28	And he said, Your name shall be called no more Jacob, but Israel: for as a prince have you power with God and with men, and have prevailed.

29	And Jacob asked *him*, and said, Tell *me*, I pray you, your name. And he said, Why *is* it *that* you do ask after my name? And he blessed him there.

30	And Jacob called the name of the place Peniel: for I have seen God face to face, and my life is preserved.

31	And as he passed over Penuel the sun rose upon him, and he halted upon his thigh.

32	Therefore the children of Israel eat not *of* the sinew which shrank, which *is* upon the hollow of the thigh, unto this day: because he touched the hollow of Jacob's thigh in the sinew that shrank.

J. Vernon McGee reminds us in his commentary on this passage that Jacob did not want to wrestle anyone. He just got out of a possible fight with Laban, his father-in-law, and was facing a possible slaughter by his twin brother. If anything, he wants to conserve his energy. But here he is fighting from the night into the early morning hours. Miserably losing. Yet, this fight teaches Jacob one all-important thing. He was in the presence of God. If he wanted to survive, he simply had to cling to God with every fiber of his being. Though his leg was broken, that pain and all the fear of what he was facing tomorrow meant nothing if he could not cling to God. Without God – all would be lost. Jacob knew this was a personal encounter with God. This is the very pre-incarnate Christ! Jacob saw Jesus face to face and was blessed because he had the sense to cling to Him. Jacob's name is now a thing of the past. He is now titled a prince, Israel, not by men, but by the King of Kings.

Dear Lord Jesus,

So often we struggle and give up, or get distracted and walk away to return to struggle again, only to walk away and return again. Lord help me to be like Israel. Help me to stand fast holding dealy onto You. May I never let You go.

In Jesus name, Amen.

DAY #89
GENESIS 33:1-11

1   And Jacob lifted up his eyes, and looked, and, behold, Esau came, and with him four hundred men. And he divided the children unto Leah, and unto Rachel, and unto the two handmaids.
2   And he put the handmaids and their children foremost, and Leah and her children after, and Rachel and Joseph hindermost.
3   And he passed over before them, and bowed himself to the ground seven times, until he came near to his brother.
4   And Esau ran to meet him, and embraced him, and fell on his neck, and kissed him: and they wept.
5   And he lifted up his eyes, and saw the women and the children; and said, Who *are* those with you? And he said, The children which God has graciously given your servant.
6   Then the handmaidens came near, they and their children, and they bowed themselves.

7   And Leah also with her children came near, and bowed themselves: and after came Joseph near and Rachel, and they bowed themselves.

8   And he said, What do you *mean* by all this drove which I met? And he said, *These are* to find grace in the sight of my lord.

9   And Esau said, I have enough, my brother; keep that you have unto yourself.

10 And Jacob said, Nay, I pray you, if now I have found grace in your sight, then receive my present at my hand: for therefore I have seen your face, as though I had seen the face of God, and you were pleased with me.

11 Take, I pray you, my blessing that is brought to you; because God has dealt graciously with me, and because I have enough. And he urged him, and he took *it*.

Esau's response to hearing Jacob's return does not give the appearance of a loving embrace to the return of his twin brother. Four hundred men swiftly approaching is nothing less than a small army. It may be that Esau upon hearing of Jacob's return was still angry. It may be that he wanted to greet his brother and embrace him. Either way, the appearance he gives is one of military strength.

Jacob, now having received God's blessings and renamed Israel, is no longer the trickster, but a man willing to face an army head-on and alone, in full humbleness with a repentant heart.

Keep in mind the large gift that was sent forward, Esau passes without stopping. He is so focused on his brother Jacob, that he pays it no attention, not even guessing that it is a gift for him, and races onward. The old Jacob, who may have thought maybe this would appease my brother is gone. Israel stands then bows seven times as he approaches an army of 400 – alone. Israel has met the

God who does impossible things. He steps forward in faith, that God will do as HE promised. That means this meeting with Esau, which must happen, must be peaceful. All Jacob's plans to address it, failed. But as Israel, as God's man, things work!

Dear Lord Jesus,

Our best-laid plans are nothing. All that we plan and do has no value without Your hand in it. Lord, cause me not to forget the importance of seeking You in all that I do, including planning my day! May the start of my day and the end of my day be filled with thoughts of Your praises. May I not allow time to seek those things which displease You. Lord, You renew my mind! You can do the impossible. Lord, strengthen me that I may praise You all the day long in all that I do.

In Jesus name, Amen.

DAY #90
GENESIS 33:12-20

12   And he said, Let us take our journey, and let us go, and I will go before you.
13   And he said unto him, My lord knows that the children *are* tender, and the flocks and herds with young *are* with me: and if men should overdrive them one day, all the flock will die.

14	Let my lord, I pray you, pass over before his servant: and I will lead on softly, according as the cattle that goes before me and the children be able to endure, until I come unto my lord unto Seir.

15	And Esau said, Let me now leave with you *some* of the folk that *are* with me. And he said, What need is there for it? let me find grace in the sight of my lord.

16	So Esau returned that day on his way unto Seir.

17	And Jacob journeyed to Succoth, and built him an house, and made booths for his cattle: therefore the name of the place is called Succoth.

18	And Jacob came to Shalem, a city of Shechem, which *is* in the land of Canaan, when he came from Padanaram; and pitched his tent before the city.

19	And he bought a parcel of a field, where he had spread his tent, at the hand of the children of Hamor, Shechem's father, for an hundred pieces of money.

20	And he erected there an altar, and called it Elohe Israel.

Esau parts from Jacob and offers an escort because the land is dangerous. Esau knows and understands the importance of a show of strength. But, from his view of Jacob, he has little if any strength. Jacob has not shown his military strength, instead, he laid down his arms. Esau seems to doubt that Jacob can survive Canaan, beyond his own personal escort, he offers the use of some of his best men to assist them in safe travel. But Jacob now trusts in GOD! What use does he have for such things, when God has promised him so much? Esau leaves and Jacob settles where he wants. He buys property, erects an altar and calls it "God of Israel."

Jacob left the land of his fathers and went to seek a wife from the land of his mother. When he left he was not living near a city.

Pay attention here. It seems Jacob forgot what his parents said about the people of this land, or he gave into temptation in the opportunities closeness to a city could bring to him.

Dear Lord Jesus,

So often the words of wisdom given to us by our parents ring true, even though we wish we even as adults were right. It seems that even as adults we cannot get away from the obvious, that it is important not only to listen to our parents but to learn from them. Lord, help me to not only take my parents' words to heart but to stand on Your Word. Lord, may Your word be a strong tower for me.

In Jesus name, Amen.

DAY #91
GENESIS 34

1   And Dinah the daughter of Leah, which she bare unto Jacob, went out to see the daughters of the land.
2   And when Shechem the son of Hamor the Hivite, prince of the country, saw her, he took her, and lay with her, and defiled her.
3   And his soul clave unto Dinah the daughter of Jacob, and he loved the damsel, and spoke kindly unto the damsel.
4   And Shechem spoke unto his father Hamor, saying, Get me this damsel to wife.

5   And Jacob heard that he had defiled Dinah his daughter: now his sons were with his cattle in the field: and Jacob held his peace until they were come.

6   And Hamor the father of Shechem went out unto Jacob to commune with him.

7   And the sons of Jacob came out of the field when they heard *it*: and the men were grieved, and they were very angry, because he had wrought folly in Israel in lying with Jacob's daughter; which thing ought not to be done.

8   And Hamor communed with them, saying, The soul of my son Shechem longs for your daughter: I pray you give her him to wife.

9   And make you marriages with us, *and* give your daughters unto us, and take our daughters unto you.

10   And you shall dwell with us: and the land shall be before you; dwell and trade you therein, and get you possessions therein.

11   And Shechem said unto her father and unto her brethren, Let me find grace in your eyes, and what you shall say unto me I will give.

12   Ask me never so much dowry and gift, and I will give according as you shall say unto me: but give me the damsel to wife.

13   And the sons of Jacob answered Shechem and Hamor his father deceitfully, and said, because he had defiled Dinah their sister:

14   And they said unto them, We cannot do this thing, to give our sister to one that is uncircumcised; for that *were* a reproach unto us:

15   But in this will we consent unto you: If you will be as we *be*, that every male of you be circumcised;

16 Then will we give our daughters unto you, and we will take your daughters to us, and we will dwell with you, and we will become one people.
17 But if you will not listen unto us, to be circumcised; then will we take our daughter, and we will be gone.
18 And their words pleased Hamor, and Shechem Hamor's son.
19 And the young man deferred not to do the thing, because he had delight in Jacob's daughter: and he *was* more honourable than all the house of his father.
20 And Hamor and Shechem his son came unto the gate of their city, and communed with the men of their city, saying,
21 These men *are* peaceable with us; therefore let them dwell in the land, and trade therein; for the land, behold, *it is* large enough for them; let us take their daughters to us for wives, and let us give them our daughters.
22 Only herein will the men consent unto us for to dwell with us, to be one people, if every male among us be circumcised, as they *are* circumcised.
23 *Shall* not their cattle and their substance and every beast of theirs *be* ours? only let us consent unto them, and they will dwell with us.
24 And unto Hamor and unto Shechem his son listened all that went out of the gate of his city; and every male was circumcised, all that went out of the gate of his city.
25 And it came to pass on the third day, when they were sore, that two of the sons of Jacob, Simeon and Levi, Dinah's brethren, took each man his sword, and came upon the city boldly, and slew all the males.
26 And they slew Hamor and Shechem his son with the edge of the sword, and took Dinah out of Shechem's house, and went out.
27 The sons of Jacob came upon the slain, and spoiled the city, because they had defiled their sister.

28 They took their sheep, and their oxen, and their asses, and that which *was* in the city, and that which *was* in the field,

29 And all their wealth, and all their little ones, and their wives took they captive, and spoiled even all that *was* in the house.

30 And Jacob said to Simeon and Levi, You have troubled me to make me to stink among the inhabitants of the land, among the Canaanites and the Perizzites: and I *being* few in number, they shall gather themselves together against me, and slay me; and I shall be destroyed, I and my house.

31 And they said, Should he deal with our sister as with an harlot?

Here we find the honesty of scripture. A horrific event combined with inaction, deceit, sinful thoughts, and acts of violence. All of these are sins of Jacob and his sons.

In a land where Esau had expressed concern that his twin brother Jacob and his family might not be safe, somehow Dinah is visiting other females without an escort! What does that say about Jacob's attentiveness to his family? What does this say about his actions as a concerned father? Was he one of those or not?

Jacob only seems to grasp his lack of awareness after Dinah pays the price. Granted nothing is said about whether Dinah left willfully without an escort having been warned, but this is still on Jacob. He was chosen by God from the womb. He was blessed, set apart, and recognized that God blessed him continually. He kept himself devoted to God while he lived amongst the idolatrous Laban. He had married two daughters of an idolator and still did not grasp the dangers of the country he returned to Dinah is raped.

Her rapist, says nice words to her after he exerted his control over her to a punishing level. This rapist then goes to his father asking for Dinah to be given to him so he can do this over and over claiming he loves her. THIS IS NOT LOVE!

Note that at no time does this passage state that the father of the rapist was aware of his son's evil. Would a father knowing his son has raped another man's daughter willingly enter the other man's fortress and commune with him while waiting for the man's 12 sons to return? If so, this father of a rapist would have entered Jacob's area believing he entered into a naïve, foolish, and defenseless man's home.

Jacob having heard that request, calls for his sons. His anger is so great he seems unable to respond in a manner that he can express. His sons come, their anger full and their desire to give their sister justice like an anchor on their souls, especially on those closest.

The words of the sons of Jacob are chosen carefully. Notice what is missing in their request for circumcision. A request that all those who wish circumcision must get rid of their idolatry is not stated! Nor is it said, you must worship God and him alone.

The sin or murder is now placed on the children of Jacob. Yet, that sin is also on Jacob. He had to grasp what was in their heart the moment they asked for circumcision.

Dear Lord Jesus,

Keep me from the desires of my heart when they are not on YOU! I want my desires to be Your desires. Yet, I know myself and openly admit to You that I allow distractions, that I allow sinful thoughts. Lord, please keep working on me! I need you to keep changing me from within. Please, Lord, finish the work You have begun in me.

In Jesus name, Amen.

DAY #92
GENESIS 35:1-2

1   And God said unto Jacob, Arise, go up to Bethel, and dwell there: and make there an altar unto God, that appeared unto you when you fled from the face of Esau your brother.
2   Then Jacob said unto his household, and to all that *were* with him, Put away the strange gods that *are* among you, and be clean, and change your garments:

SCREEEECH!

Jacob knew! He knew that there were those amongst his group who had brought idols. He knew about Rachel's sin with the idols. Were there others who brought false gods into his camp? This makes you wonder.

Jacob is the permissive father and the permissive leader. He said nothing when his oldest sons slaughtered all the men of Shechem and took their belongings after one of that city raped their sister Dinah. Jacob seems to be aware of a lot. But appears to be more of an observer than a man of action. He only dares to act when God pushes him. He says no to idols without saying anything to those who had other gods.

Dear Lord Jesus,

Strengthen my resolve to stand fast in Your Word! Embolden me to call sin – sin! Lord, remove my easy ability to stand and watch and say nothing. Make me into one known for my love of You and make my words known for reflecting Your love and words.

In Jesus name, Amen.

DAY #93
GENESIS 35:3-15

3 And let us arise, and go up to Bethel; and I will make there an altar unto God, who answered me in the day of my distress, and was with me in the way which I went.
4 And they gave unto Jacob all the strange gods which *were* in their hand, and [all their] earrings which *were* in their ears; and Jacob hid them under the oak which *was* by Shechem.
5 And they journeyed: and the terror of God was upon the cities that *were* round about them, and they did not pursue after the sons of Jacob.
6 So Jacob came to Luz, which *is* in the land of Canaan, that *is*, Bethel, he and all the people that *were* with him.
7 And he built there an altar, and called the place Elbethel: because there God appeared unto him, when he fled from the face of his brother.
8 But Deborah Rebekah's nurse died, and she was buried beneath Bethel under an oak: and the name of it was called Allonbachuth.
9 And God appeared unto Jacob again, when he came out of Padanaram, and blessed him.
10 And God said unto him, Your name *is* Jacob: your name shall not be called any more Jacob, but Israel shall be your name: and he called his name Israel.

11	And God said unto him, I *am* God Almighty: be fruitful and multiply; a nation and a company of nations shall be of you, and kings shall come out of your loins;
12	And the land which I gave Abraham and Isaac, to you I will give it, and to your seed after you will I give the land.
13	And God went up from him in the place where he talked with him.
14	And Jacob set up a pillar in the place where he talked with him, *even* a pillar of stone: and he poured a drink offering thereon, and he poured oil thereon.
15	And Jacob called the name of the place where God spoke with him, Bethel.

God wanted Jacob, to set not only his family apart from others but to include in that the removal of idolatry of all those with him, by removing the worship of false gods. Jacob's obedience to God, in moving on, soon proves to be their salvation. The nomadic lifestyle of moving towards the place God told Jacob to head to had all distractions removed, "the terror of God was upon the cities that *were* round about them." Remember that the last place Jacob settled was near a city, that bad choice made him partly responsible for what happened to his daughter.

Note that Jacob knew he had to set aside all that was not holy if he was to return to that place where God met him. He felt he was going towards a place of reverence for God's presence had been there and he expected it again. Jacob, who had met the pre-incarnate Christ, still did not fully understand God was with him all the time. Sadly, most of us don't get this message. We think we can put God aside and do whatever, then clean ourselves to meet God. That is nothing but foolishness.

Dear Lord Jesus,

You are here with me NOW! I know that I do not deserve the love you show to me in your expressed love daily and your actions dying on the cross for me. How is it You love even me? Lord, make me more like You. Work on me and make me into one who loves beyond what I am today.

In Jesus name, Amen.

DAY #94
GENESIS 35:16-21

16   And they journeyed from Bethel; and there was but a little way to come to Ephrath: and Rachel travailed, and she had hard labour.
17   And it came to pass, when she was in hard labour, that the midwife said unto her, Fear not; you shall have this son also.
18   And it came to pass, as her soul was in departing, (for she died) that she called his name Benoni: but his father called him Benjamin.
19   And Rachel died, and was buried in the way to Ephrath, which *is* Bethlehem.
20   And Jacob set a pillar upon her grave: that *is* the pillar of Rachel's grave unto this day.
21   And Israel journeyed, and spread his tent beyond the tower of Edar.

Rachel, Jacob's first love and second wife dies giving birth to Benjamin. She calls him, "Son of my sorrow." Jacob changed the name to "Son of my right hand." Jacob did not consider Benjamin Rachel's sorrow, but her crowning jewel. We know this because his name mentions the right hand.

> "And he shall set the sheep on his right hand, but the goats on the left." (Mat 25:33)

> "Jesus says unto him, Thou hast said: nevertheless I say unto you, Hereafter shall ye see the Son of man sitting on the right hand of power, and coming in the clouds of heaven." (Mat 26:64)

> "They said unto him, Grant unto us that we may sit, one on thy right hand, and the other on thy left hand, in thy glory." (Mar 10:37)

The right hand as you can see is the place of favor! Benjamin has eleven BIG brothers to watch out for him. He may not have had his mother, someone else played that role. Whether it was Leah, Rachel's sister, or Bilhah, Rachel's handmaid is not shared. Benjamin is the loved baby brother.

Dear Lord Jesus,

We often miss that which is right in front of us. We do not see or refuse to see the options you place before us, hoping we will choose you. Yet, we think in choosing wrong that tomorrow is promised. Rachel here sees tomorrow is not promised, Lord do not let me think tomorrow is promised. Push me to live as if this is it. So I may make the right choices to please YOU and not myself.

In Jesus name, Amen.

DAY #95
GENESIS 35:22-29

22　And it came to pass, when Israel dwelt in that land, that Reuben went and lay with Bilhah his father's concubine: and Israel heard *it*. Now the sons of Jacob were twelve:
23　The sons of Leah; Reuben, Jacob's firstborn, and Simeon, and Levi, and Judah, and Issachar, and Zebulun:
24　The sons of Rachel; Joseph, and Benjamin:
25　And the sons of Bilhah, Rachel's handmaid; Dan, and Naphtali:
26　And the sons of Zilpah, Leah's handmaid; Gad, and Asher: these *are* the sons of Jacob, which were born to him in Padanaram.
27　And Jacob came unto Isaac his father unto Mamre, unto the city of Arbah, which *is* Hebron, where Abraham and Isaac sojourned.
28　And the days of Isaac were an hundred and fourscore years.
29　And Isaac gave up the ghost, and died, and was gathered unto his people, *being* old and full of days: and his sons Esau and Jacob buried him.

Notice that Israel is now what Jacob is called, but when events in his past are used, his name is Jacob. His son Rueben lies with the mother of his brothers Dan and Naphtali. This is after the name change and Israel is used as his name. But to births, and to his father and brother, he is still Jacob. This brief passage says that God does not look back on what we were, but on what we will be.

Isaac dies at the age of 180. That means Jacob and Esau are 120 now. They were born when Isaac was sixty (Genesis 25:26). The next few chapters will have some overlap before this event. Both Isaac and Esau revered their father. This can be seen in how they both watch over him. Esau took on this task long before Jacob left. Remember it was Esau who was providing meat for Isaac. Jacob returns to Hebron and stays. Isaac lived 180 years. He saw his grandchildren and some of their children and more generations.

Dear Lord Jesus,

The loss of loved ones never is easy. It weighs heavily on our hearts because they are and continue to be a part of who we are. We valued their input, their smiles, and even their rebukes and chastisements. How is it Lord, we look to those we have lost and feel such a loss when their presence if brief was so important to us? Lord help those who know loss. Comfort them. Remind them that they are not alone.

In Jesus name, Amen.

DAY #96
GENESIS 36:1-43

1 Now these *are* the generations of Esau, who *is* Edom.
2 Esau took his wives of the daughters of Canaan; Adah the daughter of Elon the Hittite, and Aholibamah the daughter of Anah the daughter of Zibeon the Hivite;
3 And Bashemath Ishmael's daughter, sister of Nebajoth.
4 And Adah bare to Esau Eliphaz; and Bashemath bare Reuel;
5 And Aholibamah bare Jeush, and Jaalam, and Korah: these *are* the sons of Esau, which were born unto him in the land of Canaan.
6 And Esau took his wives, and his sons, and his daughters, and all the persons of his house, and his cattle, and all his beasts, and all his substance, which he had got in the land of Canaan; and went into the country from the face of his brother Jacob.
7 For their riches were more than that they might dwell together; and the land wherein they were strangers could not bear them because of their cattle.
8 Thus dwelt Esau in mount Seir: Esau *is* Edom.
9 And these *are* the generations of Esau the father of the Edomites in mount Seir:
10 These *are* the names of Esau's sons; Eliphaz the son of Adah the wife of Esau, Reuel the son of Bashemath the wife of Esau.
11 And the sons of Eliphaz were Teman, Omar, Zepho, and Gatam, and Kenaz.
12 And Timna was concubine to Eliphaz Esau's son; and she bare to Eliphaz Amalek: these *were* the sons of Adah Esau's wife.

13 And these *are* the sons of Reuel; Nahath, and Zerah, Shammah, and Mizzah: these were the sons of Bashemath Esau's wife.

14 And these were the sons of Aholibamah, the daughter of Anah the daughter of Zibeon, Esau's wife: and she bare to Esau Jeush, and Jaalam, and Korah.

15 These *were* dukes of the sons of Esau: the sons of Eliphaz the firstborn [son] of Esau; duke Teman, duke Omar, duke Zepho, duke Kenaz,

16 Duke Korah, duke Gatam, *and* duke Amalek: these *are* the dukes *that came* of Eliphaz in the land of Edom; these *were* the sons of Adah.

17 And these *are* the sons of Reuel Esau's son; duke Nahath, duke Zerah, duke Shammah, duke Mizzah: these *are* the dukes *that came* of Reuel in the land of Edom; these *are* the sons of Bashemath Esau's wife.

18 And these *are* the sons of Aholibamah Esau's wife; duke Jeush, duke Jaalam, duke Korah: these *were* the dukes *that came* of Aholibamah the daughter of Anah, Esau's wife.

19 These *are* the sons of Esau, who *is* Edom, and these *are* their dukes.

20 These *are* the sons of Seir the Horite, who inhabited the land; Lotan, and Shobal, and Zibeon, and Anah,

21 And Dishon, and Ezer, and Dishan: these *are* the dukes of the Horites, the children of Seir in the land of Edom.

22 And the children of Lotan were Hori and Hemam; and Lotan's sister *was* Timna.

23 And the children of Shobal *were* these; Alvan, and Manahath, and Ebal, Shepho, and Onam.

24 And these *are* the children of Zibeon; both Ajah, and Anah: this [was that] Anah that found the mules in the wilderness, as he fed the asses of Zibeon his father.

25 And the children of Anah *were* these; Dishon, and Aholibamah the daughter of Anah.
26 And these *are* the children of Dishon; Hemdan, and Eshban, and Ithran, and Cheran.
27 The children of Ezer *are* these; Bilhan, and Zaavan, and Akan.
28 The children of Dishan *are* these; Uz, and Aran.
29 These *are* the dukes *that came* of the Horites; duke Lotan, duke Shobal, duke Zibeon, duke Anah,
30 Duke Dishon, duke Ezer, duke Dishan: these *are* the dukes *that came* of Hori, among their dukes in the land of Seir.
31 And these *are* the kings that reigned in the land of Edom, before there reigned any king over the children of Israel.
32 And Bela the son of Beor reigned in Edom: and the name of his city *was* Dinhabah.
33 And Bela died, and Jobab the son of Zerah of Bozrah reigned in his stead.
34 And Jobab died, and Husham of the land of Temani reigned in his stead.
35 And Husham died, and Hadad the son of Bedad, who smote Midian in the field of Moab, reigned in his stead: and the name of his city *was* Avith.
36 And Hadad died, and Samlah of Masrekah reigned in his stead.
37 And Samlah died, and Saul of Rehoboth [by] the river reigned in his stead.
38 And Saul died, and Baalhanan the son of Achbor reigned in his stead.
39 And Baalhanan the son of Achbor died, and Hadar reigned in his stead: and the name of his city *was* Pau; and his wife's name *was* Mehetabel, the daughter of Matred, the daughter of Mezahab.

40 And these *are* the names of the dukes *that came* of Esau, according to their families, after their places, by their names; duke Timnah, duke Alvah, duke Jetheth,
41 Duke Aholibamah, duke Elah, duke Pinon,
42 Duke Kenaz, duke Teman, duke Mibzar,
43 Duke Magdiel, duke Iram: these *be* the dukes of Edom, according to their habitations in the land of their possession: he *is* Esau the father of the Edomites.

J. Vernon McGee points out that this chapter is an example of how the rejected genealogy comes before the one accepted by God. Keep in mind here that it was Esau who rejected God when he sold his birthright for food. It was Esau's love of himself and pride in his own abilities that caused him to be rejected. Jacob, now called Israel, repeatedly acknowledges that all that he has is due to God's blessings, not his own work. Even pagans around Jacob, like Laban, acknowledged this.

Esau may have had many talents, but this self-righteousness sadly leads his children to false gods. Esau's children are the first recorded nobles and royalty from the line of Abraham. This is not something they have to be proud of, it is a demonstration of the sin of lifting up the self above God. This is why God did not allow kings and queens until Saul.

Dear Lord Jesus,

I am but one, and all that I am is not due to my own efforts. All that I am is due to Your will and blessings given to me. I beg and plead that You, God Almighty, never allow my children to think of themselves as above You. Remove any sense of self-superiority so that they may seek Your face and call upon You as their Lord.

In Jesus name, Amen.

DAY #97
GENESIS 37:1-4

1   And Jacob dwelt in the land wherein his father was a stranger, in the land of Canaan.
2   These *are* the generations of Jacob. Joseph, *being* seventeen years old, was feeding the flock with his brethren; and the lad *was* with the sons of Bilhah, and with the sons of Zilpah, his father's wives: and Joseph brought unto his father their evil report.
3   Now Israel loved Joseph more than all his children, because he *was* the son of his old age: and he made him a coat of *many* colours.
4   And when his brethren saw that their father loved him more than all his brethren, they hated him, and could not speak peaceably unto him.

Joseph is seventeen years old, Benjamin, his little brother is about a year old now. His father Israel, is now 108 and his grandfather Isaac is 168. Isaac does not die until he is 180. Joseph at seventeen is the youngest brother not under the watchful eye of a mother figure. Like most baby brothers, he wants to be like his big brothers. He has been the willing tag-a-long while the older brothers look back and often wish they did not have the responsibility of looking after him. Even with him at the age of seventeen, they are tired of this responsibility. Joseph the eager and honest child, brings to his father an evil report from his brothers. We are not told what that report was. Perhaps it was a message they wanted given to test just how favored Joseph was, then when they had delivered such a message to their father.

Note that Israel was living close to his father Isaac, who played favorites with his sons. Israel gives his seventeen-year-old a gift he has not given to any other son – a coat of many colors. This is a gift made by their father! A gift their father made by his own hand. The jealousy that was growing from this favored attention was reaching a peak.

Fathers, we have to be men of fairness, not men that play favorites. We make a good many mistakes. But this is one that if we do make we should correct immediately. This is not something easy to do. It takes time to and honest admission of wrongdoing and ask forgiveness. Do we as men seeking to do HIS will want our children to see us as playing favorites, or do we want our children to see us as honestly seeking HIS will and willing to admit our own sins?

Dear Lord Jesus,

I am a sinner You saved. You have changed my entire life with Your love for me. I want this love You have for me to reach beyond me to my children and their children. I want those around me to know this love. It is infectious. It needs to be shared. Lord embolden me! Make me stronger and more daring to share this love each day.

In Jesus name, Amen.

DAY #99
GENESIS 37:5-11

5   And Joseph dreamed a dream, and he told *it* his brethren: and they hated him yet the more.
6   And he said unto them, Hear, I pray you, this dream which I have dreamed:
7   For, behold, we *were* binding sheaves in the field, and, lo, my sheaf arose, and also stood upright; and, behold, your sheaves stood round about, and bowed to my sheaf.
8   And his brethren said to him, Shall you indeed reign over us? or shall you indeed have dominion over us? And they hated him yet the more for his dreams, and for his words.
9   And he dreamed yet another dream, and told it his brethren, and said, Behold, I have dreamed a dream more; and, behold, the sun and the moon and the eleven stars bowed to me.
10 And he told *it* to his father, and to his brethren: and his father rebuked him, and said unto him, What *is* this dream that you have dreamed? Shall I and your mother and your brethren indeed come to bow down ourselves to you to the earth?
11 And his brethren envied him; but his father observed the saying.

Joseph has received a prophecy. A dream which stays with him, a dream he must share. Part of the reason is it brings him happiness to share it, but it is not clear if he understood what the dreams meant. The interpretation was very clear and simple to his brothers and to his father. The dreams told them, this seventeen-year-old, soon-to-be man would reign over them. Remember the immediacy in which this is seen and the context in which it is shared. Joseph, the tag-a-long little brother, one of the two youngest and one of the favored children, shared a dream where it seemed he was given power over them. The second dream even had the sun and moon, representing his mother and father bowing to him. But, what if the dreams were actually a bit deeper in meaning. In the first dream, the sheaves bow. A sheaf is a bundle of grain bound together. Thinking on this, the coming feminine has importance also. What if the sheaves represent their offspring? Why would all bow to Joseph? Because Jesus the Messiah is Joseph's descendant!

Dear Lord Jesus,

You are so patient with us. We get things wrong, sometimes on purpose. We don't listen. We refuse to follow directions, and still You are there waiting for us to call on Your name. You never leave us. You walk with us through all our trials and joys. Lord, let me praise you with not only who I am, but how I live and what words I choose.

In Jesus name, Amen.

DAY #99
GENESIS 37:12-36

12   And his brethren went to feed their father's flock in Shechem.
13   And Israel said unto Joseph, Do not your brethren feed *the flock* in Shechem? come, and I will send you unto them. And he said to him, Here *am I*.
14   And he said to him, Go, I pray you, see whether it be well with your brethren, and well with the flocks; and bring me word again. So he sent him out of the vale of Hebron, and he came to Shechem.
15   And a certain man found him, and, behold, *he was* wandering in the field: and the man asked him, saying, What do you seek?
16   And he said, I seek my brethren: tell me, I pray you, where they feed *their flocks*.
17   And the man said, They are departed hence; for I heard them say, Let us go to Dothan. And Joseph went after his brethren, and found them in Dothan.
18   And when they saw him afar off, even before he came near unto them, they conspired against him to slay him.
19   And they said one to another, Behold, this dreamer comes.
20   Come now therefore, and let us slay him, and cast him into some pit, and we will say, Some evil beast has devoured him: and we shall see what will become of his dreams.
21   And Reuben heard *it*, and he delivered him out of their hands; and said, Let us not kill him.
22   And Reuben said unto them, Shed no blood, *but* cast him into this pit that *is* in the wilderness, and lay no hand upon him; that he might rid him out of their hands, to deliver him to his father again.

23   And it came to pass, when Joseph was come unto his brethren, that they stripped Joseph out of his coat, *his* coat of *many* colours that *was* on him;

24   And they took him, and cast him into a pit: and the pit *was* empty, *there was* no water in it.

25   And they sat down to eat bread: and they lifted up their eyes and looked, and, behold, a company of Ishmaelites came from Gilead with their camels bearing spicery and balm and myrrh, going to carry *it* down to Egypt.

26   And Judah said unto his brethren, What profit *is it* if we slay our brother, and conceal his blood?

27   Come, and let us sell him to the Ishmaelites, and let not our hand be upon him; for he *is* our brother *and* our flesh. And his brethren were content.

28   Then there passed by Midianites merchantmen; and they drew and lifted up Joseph out of the pit, and sold Joseph to the Ishmaelites for twenty *pieces* of silver: and they brought Joseph into Egypt.

29   And Reuben returned unto the pit; and, behold, Joseph *was* not in the pit; and he rent his clothes.

30   And he returned unto his brethren, and said, The child *is* not; and I, where shall I go?

31   And they took Joseph's coat, and killed a kid of the goats, and dipped the coat in the blood;

32   And they sent the coat of *many* colours, and they brought *it* to their father; and said, This have we found: know now whether it *be* your son's coat or no.

33   And he knew it, and said, *it is* my son's coat; an evil beast has devoured him; Joseph is without doubt rent in pieces.

34   And Jacob rent his clothes, and put sackcloth upon his loins, and mourned for his son many days.

35   And all his sons and all his daughters rose up to comfort him; but he refused to be comforted; and he said, For I will

go down into the grave unto my son mourning. Thus his father wept for him.

36   And the Midianites sold him into Egypt unto Potiphar, an officer of Pharaoh's, *and* captain of the guard.

Why does Reuben say no to killing Joseph? Because Reuben has been granted mercy by his father, for his sin of adultery against his very own father. His father could have had him killed. But through mercy, he was allowed to live. Reuben is the oldest. He is the leader. But this time he walks away from that responsibility leaving Jacob's life in their hands. When he returns from whatever he choose to do in order to not be responsible, he finds his baby brother Joseph – gone. His brothers sold their own brother into slavery. They get twenty pieces of silver. Enough for them each to have two pieces of silver.

They made a profit from selling their prophet brother. Whose dreams set himself above them. The favoritism, Joseph's dreams, who justified their sale right? They soon learned after returning that a parent's loss of a child is inconsolable. Nothing stops a parent from sorrow over the loss of a child. It breaks a parent's heart. They conveyed this story to their father with the possibility that Joseph could still be alive. But delivered it with a bloody coat. They were responsible for all that would come.

Dear Lord Jesus,

How do I, a sinner, matter so much to You? I was deep in my sins before You called me! Why is it that You chose me? How can I be so loved? What did I do to deserve this – this love that is unending? Lord, make me into a better person. I do not believe I am capable of such a love. Your mercies are new every morning. Keep working on me. I want to be more like You!

In Jesus name, Amen.

DAY #100
GENESIS 38

1 And it came to pass at that time, that Judah went down from his brethren, and turned in to a certain Adullamite, whose name *was* Hirah.
2 And Judah saw there a daughter of a certain Canaanite, whose name *was* Shuah; and he took her, and went in unto her.
3 And she conceived, and bare a son; and he called his name Er.
4 And she conceived again, and bare a son; and she called his name Onan.
5 And she yet again conceived, and bare a son; and called his name Shelah: and he was at Chezib, when she bare him.
6 And Judah took a wife for Er his firstborn, whose name *was* Tamar.
7 And Er, Judah's firstborn, was wicked in the sight of the LORD; and the LORD slew him.
8 And Judah said unto Onan, Go in unto your brother's wife, and marry her, and raise up seed to your brother.
9 And Onan knew that the seed should not be his; and it came to pass, when he went in unto his brother's wife, that he spilled *it* on the ground, lest that he should give seed to his brother.

10 And the thing which he did displeased the LORD: why he slew him also.

11 Then said Judah to Tamar his daughter in law, Remain a widow at your father's house, till Shelah my son be grown: for he said, Lest peradventure he die also, as his brethren *did*. And Tamar went and dwelt in her father's house.

12 And in process of time the daughter of Shuah Judah's wife died; and Judah was comforted, and went up unto his sheepshearers to Timnath, he and his friend Hirah the Adullamite.

13 And it was told Tamar, saying, Behold your father in law goes up to Timnath to shear his sheep.

14 And she put her widow's garments off from her, and covered her with a vail, and wrapped herself, and sat in an open place, which *is* by the way to Timnath; for she saw that Shelah was grown, and she was not given unto him to wife.

15 When Judah saw her, he thought her *to be* an harlot; because she had covered her face.

16 And he turned unto her by the way, and said, Go to, I pray you, let me come in unto you; (for he knew not that she *was* his daughter in law.) And she said, What *will* you give me, that you mayest come in unto me?

17 And he said, I will send *you* a kid from the flock. And she said, *Will* you give *me* a pledge, till you send *it*?

18 And he said, What pledge shall I give you? And she said, Your signet, and your bracelets, and your staff that *is* in your hand. And he gave *it* her, and came in unto her, and she conceived by him.

19 And she arose, and went away, and laid by her vail from her, and put on the garments of her widowhood.

20 And Judah sent the kid by the hand of his friend the Adullamite, to receive *his* pledge from the woman's hand: but he found her not.

21 Then he asked the men of that place, saying, Where *is* the harlot, that *was* openly by the way side? And they said, There was no harlot in this *place*.

22 And he returned to Judah, and said, I cannot find her; and also the men of the place said, *that* there was no harlot in this *place*.

23 And Judah said, Let her take *it* to her, lest we be shamed: behold, I sent this kid, and you have not found her.

24 And it came to pass about three months after, that it was told Judah, saying, Tamar your daughter in law has played the harlot; and also, behold, she *is* with child by whoredom. And Judah said, Bring her forth, and let her be burnt.

25 When she *was* brought forth, she sent to her father in law, saying, By the man, whose these *are, am* I with child: and she said, Discern, I pray you, whose *are* these, the signet, and bracelets, and staff.

26 And Judah acknowledged *them*, and said, She has been more righteous than I; because that I gave her not to Shelah my son. And he knew her again no more.

27 And it came to pass in the time of her travail, that, behold, twins *were* in her womb.

28 And it came to pass, when she travailed, that *the one* put out *his* hand: and the midwife took and bound upon his hand a scarlet thread, saying, This came out first.

29 And it came to pass, as he drew back his hand, that, behold, his brother came out: and she said, How have you broken forth? *this* breach *be* upon you: therefore his name was called Pharez.

30 And afterward came out his brother, that had the scarlet thread upon his hand: and his name was called Zarah.

A first glance at this passage makes you think why is this even here? The truth is that it is for two reasons. Jesus is the LION OF THE TRIBE OF JUDAH. This shows his lineage. Matthew cites some of the names listed here. The second reason is that it is a statement, that even though Joseph was sold into slavery, life goes on. God did not stop being God, because Joseph, his point man was sold off. God was the witness to Judah's sins and the sins of his children.

J. Vernon McGee points out what a negligent father Israel had to be to NOT RAISE UP all of his children in the way they should go. Ten of his children he neglected. He was ambivalent and permissive. He is an example of the absent father, even though he was present. What a horrible example of how to be a good father to all. Dads out there, be involved in your children's lives.

Dear Lord Jesus,

Thank you for good friendships that help us to stand stronger with You! Thank you for Your being there with me through everything never once leaving me alone. Lord, may You be praised for You do not change! Even though life goes on, You are the one and only constant we can trust to remain the same. Praise be to You, the Most High God!

In Jesus name, Amen.

DAY #101
GENESIS 39:1-5

1 And Joseph was brought down to Egypt; and Potiphar, an officer of Pharaoh, captain of the guard, an Egyptian, bought him of the hands of the Ishmaelites, which had brought him down thither.
2 And the LORD was with Joseph, and he was a prosperous man; and he was in the house of his master the Egyptian.
3 And his master saw that the LORD *was* with him, and that the LORD made all that he did to prosper in his hand.
4 And Joseph found grace in his sight, and he served him: and he made him overseer over his house, and all *that* he had he put into his hand.
5 And it came to pass from the time *that* he had made him overseer in his house, and over all that he had, that the LORD blessed the Egyptian's house for Joseph's sake; and the blessing of the LORD was upon all that he had in the house, and in the field.

Joseph, though a slave still seeks God. This shows that Israel's favoritism towards Joseph and Benjamin allowed Joseph to imitate his father's devotion to God. His habits are carried into Joseph's captivity. Not here that nothing is said of Joseph's habits, but it is seen that his hard work is blessed by God. Joseph does not whine about being sold. He seems to have accepted what some may call "his fate" to be a slave. He is resolved to give his best and to continue to serve God, no matter where he is.

The last chapter has about 20 years if not more. This chapter has no hints as to how long Joseph serves Potiphar.

Dear Lord Jesus,

How do we give our best no matter what we are dealt in life? This is a struggle within ourselves. Lord, help me to not be one to give in to sin, Strengthen my resolve to serve You and You alone. Remove the temptations and the foolish nature that makes me think my sins do not matter. Lord, You gave all for me. I want to be like You. Work on me – make me able to be like You so that I may give all for You.

In Jesus name, Amen.

DAY #102
GENESIS 39:6-20

6   And he left all that he had in Joseph's hand; and he knew not ought he had, save the bread which he did eat. And Joseph was *a* goodly *person*, and well favoured.
7   And it came to pass after these things, that his master's wife cast her eyes upon Joseph; and she said, Lie with me.
8   But he refused, and said unto his master's wife, Behold, my master does not know what *is* with me in the house, and he has committed all that he has to my hand;
9   *There is* none greater in this house than I; neither has he kept back any thing from me but you, because you *are* his wife: how then can I do this great wickedness, and sin against God?
10 And it came to pass, as she spoke to Joseph day by day, that he listened not unto her, to lie by her, *or* to be with her.

11 And it came to pass about this time, that *Joseph* went into the house to do his business; and *there was* none of the men of the house there within.

12 And she caught him by his garment, saying, Lie with me: and he left his garment in her hand, and fled, and got him out.

13 And it came to pass, when she saw that he had left his garment in her hand, and was fled forth,

14 That she called unto the men of her house, and spoke unto them, saying, See, he has brought in an Hebrew unto us to mock us; he came in unto me to lie with me, and I cried with a loud voice:

15 And it came to pass, when he heard that I lifted up my voice and cried, that he left his garment with me, and fled, and got him out.

16 And she laid up his garment by her, until his lord came home.

17 And she spoke unto him according to these words, saying, The Hebrew servant, which you have brought unto us, came in unto me to mock me:

18 And it came to pass, as I lifted up my voice and cried, that he left his garment with me, and fled out.

19 And it came to pass, when his master heard the words of his wife, which she spoke unto him, saying, After this manner did your servant to me; that his wrath was kindled.

20 And Joseph's master took him, and put him into the prison, a place where the king's prisoners *were* bound: and he was there in the prison.

FLEE TEMPTATION!! Run like the wind! Do not care what you leave behind! Joseph was a slave. He had little to show for his hard labor because he was property. He was fired and jailed for doing nothing but fleeing temptation. He kept his Master's wife untouched by his hands by refusing her and running. This man did not question his wife's word. As a result, he loses the blessings Joseph's presence brought.

When things seem awful, they seem all going wrong, could it be that this too is God? As much as we hate this concept, the answer is yes. God is with us when the horrible happens. The death of a child, the murders of loved ones, the loss of property, and these are horrible things to live through, yet the truth is God is there with us through these things and has something better for us. Where we land is because of God. Joseph found himself in jail. We have no idea how old he is, but he is no longer the naïve teenager. He is a man who understands he just needs to do what God asks of him. Isn't this what we should be thinking?

Dear Lord Jesus,

You see us through trials and tribulations. You bring us through the most horrific things. We may see tomorrow as not a sign of something good coming. But You are there to show us the sunrise! Lord, strengthen me that I may ask, "What do You want me to do today?" Press me forward that I may share Your love more each day.

In Jesus name, Amen.

DAY #103
GENESIS 39:21-23

21 But the LORD was with Joseph, and shown him mercy, and gave him favour in the sight of the keeper of the prison.
22 And the keeper of the prison committed to Joseph's hand all the prisoners that *were* in the prison; and whatsoever they did there, he was the doer *of it.*
23 The keeper of the prison looked not to any thing *that was* under his hand; because the LORD was with him, and *that* which he did, the LORD made *it* to prosper.

Let us not forget that God knows where you are. Whether you are in prison or in a mansion, God knows where you are! If you are doing what God asks of you, you are not promised an easy life anywhere in scripture! If anything Joseph's life serves as an example of this. He is blessed, and those around him who do not believe, see it. What amazes me about this, is that we do not have a record of those who see who witness this blessing upon Joseph, asking how to serve his God.

But again, Christians are not told that choosing to follow Christ will bring them an easier life anywhere in the Bible. We are promised instead of persecution. Joseph was beaten, sold into slavery, and then thrown into prison. All for doing what God asked of him.

Dear Lord Jesus,

I serve You not because of what You can give me. I serve You because of what You have already done for me. You shed Your blood that I might have life. I have to share this love. I have to tell others of its greatness. Lord, make me stronger in this. Empower me to be a better example of Your love so that others may see what You have already done for them.

In Jesus name, Amen.

DAY #104
GENESIS 40:1-8

1   And it came to pass after these things, *that* the butler of the king of Egypt and *his* baker had offended their lord the king of Egypt.
2   And Pharaoh was angered against two *of* his officers, against the chief of the butlers, and against the chief of the bakers.
3   And he put them in ward in the house of the captain of the guard, into the prison, the place where Joseph *was* bound.
4   And the captain of the guard charged Joseph with them, and he served them: and they continued a season in ward.
5   And they dreamed a dream both of them, each man his dream in one night, each man according to the interpretation of his dream, the butler and the baker of the king of Egypt, which *were* bound in the prison.
6   And Joseph came in unto them in the morning, and looked upon them, and, behold, they *were* sad.
7   And he asked Pharaoh's officers that *were* with him in the ward of his lord's house, saying, Why do you look *so* sadly to day?

8 And they said unto him, We have dreamed a dream, and *There is* no interpreter of it. And Joseph said unto them, *Do* not interpretations *belong* to God? tell me *them*, I pray you.

God is the best planner! Joseph was enslaved by his brothers, sold to Potiphar, raised to a position of power, imprisoned for a crime he didn't commit, and entrusted with an allowed supervision status. Then, he had two royal servants placed under him, and he served them. Some may think Joseph didn't grasp the job he was given of supervision. The Bible clearly states, "And the captain of the guard charged Joseph with them, **and he served them**...." Servants with a servant, of all places in prison! But Joseph was a slave who is lower than a servant right? Remember who was put in charge. How long did it take for Joseph to earn the respect and position he was given in prison? How long did it take for the two servants to entrust their personal dreams to Joseph? God made Joseph humble to be ready for these two men. From the favored son to a prisoner for something he did not do, to a supervisor who believes leading is all about serving. God arranged this perfect timing. He put all the pieces together for this moment and more.

Think about moments in your life when someone suddenly was there for you. How many streetlights did they have to pass through to get there at that exact moment? How many people did the pass to get to you at that exact moment? God loves you! He arranged that time because He loves you! Guess what? God is still planning things for you!

Dear Lord Jesus,

I will never grasp how much you do for me. Strengthen my resolve to do what You desire. Strengthen me each day through the reading of Your Word, that I may be a better person toward those who know me best.

In Jesus name, Amen.

DAY #105
GENESIS 40:9-23

9   And the chief butler told his dream to Joseph, and said to him, In my dream, behold, a vine *was* before me;
10 And in the vine *were* three branches: and it *was* as though it budded, *and* her blossoms shot forth; and the clusters thereof brought forth ripe grapes:
11 And Pharaoh's cup *was* in my hand: and I took the grapes, and pressed them into Pharaoh's cup, and I gave the cup into Pharaoh's hand.
12 And Joseph said unto him, This *is* the interpretation of it: The three branches *are* three days:
13 Yet within three days shall Pharaoh lift up your head, and restore you unto your place: and you shall deliver Pharaoh's cup into his hand, after the former manner when you were his butler.
14 But think on me when it shall be well with you, and shew kindness, I pray you, unto me, and make mention of me unto Pharaoh, and bring me out of this house:

15 For indeed I was stolen away out of the land of the Hebrews: and here also have I done nothing that they should put me into the dungeon.
16 When the chief baker saw that the interpretation was good, he said unto Joseph, I also *was* in my dream, and, behold, *I had* three white baskets on my head:
17 And in the uppermost basket *there was* of all manner of bakemeats for Pharaoh; and the birds did eat them out of the basket upon my head.
18 And Joseph answered and said, This *is* the interpretation thereof: The three baskets *are* three days:
19 Yet within three days shall Pharaoh lift up your head from off you, and shall hang you on a tree; and the birds shall eat your flesh from off you.
20 And it came to pass the third day, *which was* Pharaoh's birthday, that he made a feast unto all his servants: and he lifted up the head of the chief butler and of the chief baker among his servants.
21 And he restored the chief butler unto his butlership again; and he gave the cup into Pharaoh's hand:
22 But he hanged the chief baker: as Joseph had interpreted to them.
23 Yet did not the chief butler remember Joseph, but forgot him.

It is interesting here that the two royal servants placed under Joseph both had opportunities to poison the Pharaoh's food. Their imprisonment seems to have been temporary while an investigation was done. This would explain the dreams, their interpretations, and the pinpoint accuracy of Joseph's words as he gave credit to God for the knowledge.

Joseph was 100 percent accurate. But it is Joseph who credits God for interpreting the dream. This could have been a hint to the butler and baker, "Get closer to God" and such things may be granted to you.

The forgetting of Joseph may have been caused by two things. One, royal servant etiquette, who did not allow him an opportunity to share with the Pharaoh. Two, that God wanted the perfect time for this information to be revealed. Knowledge is power is something we teach to children. But obtaining information at the time it is needed most is rare. This was all about God's perfect timing!

Dear Lord Jesus,

You put things together in ways we have to sit back and marvel. Lord, You do things in the perfect time. Lord, there are many wanted things now. I admit I am one of them. I want this and that and I want it now! Lord, forgive me. I know Your timing is always best. Lord, let me praise You at every opportunity for Your glorious planning.

In Jesus name, Amen.

DAY #106
GENESIS 41:1-14

1   And it came to pass at the end of two full years, that Pharaoh dreamed: and, behold, he stood by the river.

2   And, behold, there came up out of the river seven well favoured cows and fatfleshed; and they fed in a meadow.

3   And, behold, seven other cows came up after them out of the river, ill favoured and lean-fleshed; and stood by the *other* cows upon the brink of the river.

4   And the ill favoured and lean-fleshed cows did eat up the seven well favoured and fat cows. So Pharaoh awoke.

5   And he slept and dreamed the second time: and, behold, seven ears of corn came up upon one stalk, rank and good.

6   And, behold, seven thin ears and blasted with the east wind sprung up after them.

7   And the seven thin ears devoured the seven rank and full ears. And Pharaoh awoke, and, behold, *it was* a dream.

8   And it came to pass in the morning that his spirit was troubled; and he sent and called for all the magicians of Egypt, and all the wise men thereof: and Pharaoh told them his dream; but *there was* none that could interpret them unto Pharaoh.

9   Then spoke the chief butler unto Pharaoh, saying, I do remember my faults this day:

10 Pharaoh was wroth with his servants, and put me in ward in the captain of the guard's house, *both* me and the chief baker:

11 And we dreamed a dream in one night, I and he; we dreamed each man according to the interpretation of his dream.

12 And *there was* there with us a young man, an Hebrew, servant to the captain of the guard; and we told him, and he interpreted to us our dreams; to each man according to his dream he did interpret.

13 And it came to pass, as he interpreted to us, so it was; me he restored unto mine office, and him he hanged.

14   Then Pharaoh sent and called Joseph, and they brought him hastily out of the dungeon: and he shaved *himself*, and changed his raiment, and came in unto Pharaoh.

Can you imagine being the butler at this time and realizing your forgetfulness of someone who set your mind at ease through interpreting your dream, you somehow forgot until now? Maybe there was not a good moment to say anything, but now is the perfect time to talk about the Hebrew prisoner, Joseph.

It is as if there are a bunch of puzzle pieces on the table and suddenly they begin to be put together. The butler has to be questioned if he went to jail because he was supposed to meet Joseph. The Pharaoh has to be asking himself did he sent a man to jail so he could meet Joseph when he needed him two years later.

During all this time one thing was constant. Joseph lived as God wanted him. He pursued God's will even though it seems he was forgotten. Joseph was faithful. He was ready and willing to do whatever God set for him to do. Isn't this how we should greet each day?

Dear Lord Jesus,

You are great and mighty. You are the great planner above which there is none. Lord Jesus, strengthen me in my daily walk, that I may be more faithful like Joseph being ready to serve and aid others. Lord, use me and the way I live my life to bring others to You.

In Jesus name, Amen.

DAY #107
GENESIS 41:15-32

15   And Pharaoh said unto Joseph, I have dreamed a dream, and *There is* none that can interpret it: and I have heard say of you, *that* you canst understand a dream to interpret it.
16   And Joseph answered Pharaoh, saying, *it is* not in me: God shall give Pharaoh an answer of peace.
17   And Pharaoh said unto Joseph, In my dream, behold, I stood upon the bank of the river:
18   And, behold, there came up out of the river seven cows, fat-fleshed and well favoured; and they fed in a meadow:
19   And, behold, seven other cows came up after them, poor and very ill favoured and lean-fleshed, such as I never saw in all the land of Egypt for badness:
20   And the lean and the ill favoured cows did eat up the first seven fat cows:
21   And when they had eaten them up, it could not be known that they had eaten them; but they *were* still ill favoured, as at the beginning. So I awoke.
22   And I saw in my dream, and, behold, seven ears came up in one stalk, full and good:
23   And, behold, seven ears, withered, thin, *and* blasted with the east wind, sprung up after them:
24   And the thin ears devoured the seven good ears: and I told *this* unto the magicians; but *there was* none that could declare *it* to me.
25   And Joseph said unto Pharaoh, The dream of Pharaoh *is* one: God has shown Pharaoh what he *is* about to do.

26 The seven good cows *are* seven years; and the seven good ears *are* seven years: the dream *is* one.
27 And the seven thin and ill favoured cows that came up after them *are* seven years; and the seven empty ears blasted with the east wind shall be seven years of famine.
28 This *is* the thing which I have spoken unto Pharaoh: What God *is* about to do he shows unto Pharaoh.
29 Behold, there come seven years of great plenty throughout all the land of Egypt:
30 And there shall arise after them seven years of famine; and all the plenty shall be forgotten in the land of Egypt; and the famine shall consume the land;
31 And the plenty shall not be known in the land by reason of that famine following; for it *shall be* very grievous.
32 And for that the dream was doubled unto Pharaoh twice; *it is* because the thing *is* established by God, and God will shortly bring it to pass.

The interpretation of the dream is now complete. This explains all of why God's planning, His perfectness in this need to be seen. The time indeed is very short before this dream comes to pass. God put HIS choice of man to interpret the pharaoh's dream in a place easily reachable and within his power to do so. It cost Pharaoh nothing. What Pharaoh achieved was more than peace of mind. He was able to protect his people. Think about this God sent a troubling dream, Not one but two. To stress the immediacy of the situation. Add onto that, God placed an uneasiness, and anxiety over the rush to get this dream interpreted so that the solution could be applied in a timely manner so that no one would go hungry. This would save not only Egypt but unite Israel once again.

Dear Lord Jesus,

You see what I cannot. You plan for what I cannot predict. You guide my steps when I step into the unknown. Lord, prepare my heart. Help me to trust and believe greater than ever before.

In Jesus name, Amen.

DAY #108
GENESIS 41:33-46

33   Now therefore let Pharaoh look out a man discreet and wise, and set him over the land of Egypt.
34   Let Pharaoh do *this*, and let him appoint officers over the land, and take up the fifth part of the land of Egypt in the seven plenteous years.
35   And let them gather all the food of those good years that come, and lay up corn under the hand of Pharaoh, and let them keep food in the cities.
36   And that food shall be for store to the land against the seven years of famine, which shall be in the land of Egypt; that the land perish not through the famine.
37   And the thing was good in the eyes of Pharaoh, and in the eyes of all his servants.
38   And Pharaoh said unto his servants, Can we find *such a one* as this *is*, a man in whom the Spirit of God *is*?
39   And Pharaoh said unto Joseph, Forasmuch as God has shown you all this, *There is* none so discreet and wise as you *are*:

40	You shall be over my house, and according unto your word shall all my people be ruled: only in the throne will I be greater than you.
41	And Pharaoh said unto Joseph, See, I have set you over all the land of Egypt.
42	And Pharaoh took off his ring from his hand, and put it upon Joseph's hand, and arrayed him in vestures of fine linen, and put a gold chain about his neck;
43	And he made him to ride in the second chariot which he had; and they cried before him, Bow the knee: and he made him *ruler* over all the land of Egypt.
44	And Pharaoh said unto Joseph, I *am* Pharaoh, and without you shall no man lift up his hand or foot in all the land of Egypt.
45	And Pharaoh called Joseph's name Zaphnathpaaneah; and he gave him to wife Asenath the daughter of Potipherah priest of On. And Joseph went out over *all* the land of Egypt.
46	And Joseph *was* thirty years old when he stood before Pharaoh king of Egypt. And Joseph went out from the presence of Pharaoh, and went throughout all the land of Egypt.

Joseph did not only give an interpretation of the dream. He told Pharaoh how he should respond to the dream. So many are quick to point out a problem. Few provide a solution to a problem. Joseph provides Pharaoh with the solution needed to achieve a good and safe outcome through a seven-year drought!

Joseph had been a slave and in prison for thirteen years before he faced Pharaoh. God sharpened him, improved him, and refined him for that encounter. Joseph was no longer naïve. He was aware of the world around him. He was careful with his word choice. He understood being under authority in a new context of humbleness.

The response of Pharaoh demonstrates Joseph's humble delivery of wisdom was also one of bold delivery. Few men would stand before a man and tell him of a coming tragedy such as a seven-year drought and expect to walk away. Joseph gives credit to God first! Pharaoh does not miss this. He notices it as the reason that Joseph is able to provide the solution. Pharaoh gives him the best he cannot to promote himself, but to protect his people.

Dear Lord Jesus,

Thank you for showing me that You continually work on us, and bring us to a point of being useful. Lord, keep refining me. I need Your guiding hand to direct me where I should go and where I should not. Lord, help me to seek You first and foremost and to avoid distractions in my pursuit of You.

In Jesus name, Amen.

DAY #109
GENESIS 41:47-57

47   And in the seven plenteous years the earth brought forth by handfuls.
48   And he gathered up all the food of the seven years, which were in the land of Egypt, and laid up the food in the cities:

49 the food of the field, which *was* round about every city, laid he up in the same.
49 And Joseph gathered corn as the sand of the sea, very much, until he left numbering; for *it was* without number.
50 And unto Joseph were born two sons before the years of famine came, which Asenath the daughter of Potipherah priest of On bare unto him.
51 And Joseph called the name of the firstborn Manasseh: For God, *said* he, has made me forget all my toil, and all my father's house.
52 And the name of the second called he Ephraim: For God has caused me to be fruitful in the land of my affliction.
53 And the seven years of plenteousness, that was in the land of Egypt, were ended.
54 And the seven years of dearth began to come, according as Joseph had said: and scarcity was in all lands; but in all the land of Egypt there was bread.
55 And when all the land of Egypt was famished, the people cried to Pharaoh for bread: and Pharaoh said unto all the Egyptians, Go unto Joseph; what he says to you, do.
56 And the famine was over all the face of the earth: And Joseph opened all the storehouses, and sold unto the Egyptians; and the famine waxed sore in the land of Egypt.
57 And all countries came into Egypt to Joseph for to buy *corn*; because that the famine was *so* sore in all lands.

Joseph was blessed so much as he worked in those first seven years, that he named his children Manasseh (God made him forget all his toil) and Ephraim (God caused me to be fruitful in the land of his affliction). God blessed Joseph so much as he worked to save not only Egypt but the surrounding territories, that Joseph forgot his time as a slave and as a prisoner. Joseph did not dwell on the past. He lived in the present. He did not worry about the future, because God took care of that with HIS warnings to Pharaoh.

Pharaoh kept his word to Joseph. He indeed put Joseph in charge and reaped the benefits of Joseph's devotion to God and the wisdom God granted him. This singular choice by Pharaoh likely would have seemed harsh to those who were farmers at first. Unbelief likely would have resulted in some rebellion, but the moment things went bad. Can you imagine the joy and claims of greatness he must have received for putting the right man in that post. But we both know it wasn't Pharaoh who put him there. God groomed Joseph for just that moment.

We should learn from God's actions and Joseph's attitude about life. Live in the present, not the past. Trust God to direct our paths and things will be better. Keep in mind Joseph went through slavery and imprisonment. This is not a promise of no bad things.

Dear Lord Jesus,

Thank you for the example of Joseph on how to live life living in the present. Put my mind on the present not on the things of the past I have done wrong, nor on a future I cannot know. Help me to make the best choices for today! Help me to see that what happens today is far more important than anything in the past or that may be in the future. Today is the moment I have to make choices. Today is the time I am living. For this, I owe You my life. You have saved me in multiple ways. Lord make me into a living testimony of your love.

In Jesus name, Amen.

DAY #110
GENESIS 42:1-20

1 Now when Jacob saw that there was corn in Egypt, Jacob said unto his sons, Why do you look one upon another?
2 And he said, Behold, I have heard that there is corn in Egypt: go down there, and buy for us from there; that we may live, and not die.
3 And Joseph's ten brethren went down to buy corn in Egypt.
4 But Benjamin, Joseph's brother, Jacob sent not with his brethren; for he said, Lest peradventure mischief befall him.
5 And the sons of Israel came to buy *corn* among those that came: for the famine was in the land of Canaan.
6 And Joseph *was* the governor over the land, *and* he *it was* that sold to all the people of the land: and Joseph's brethren came, and bowed down themselves before him *with* their faces to the earth.
7 And Joseph saw his brethren, and he knew them, but made himself strange unto them, and spoke roughly unto them; and he said unto them, Where do you come from? And they said, From the land of Canaan to buy food.
8 And Joseph knew his brethren, but they knew not him.
9 And Joseph remembered the dreams which he dreamed of them, and said unto them, You *are* spies; to see the nakedness of the land you are come.
10 And they said unto him, Nay, my lord, but to buy food are your servants come.
11 We *are* all one man's sons; we *are* true *men*, your servants are no spies.

12   And he said unto them, Nay, but to see the nakedness of the land you are come.
13   And they said, Your servants *are* twelve brethren, the sons of one man in the land of Canaan; and, behold, the youngest *is* this day with our father, and one *is* not.
14   And Joseph said unto them, That *is it* that I spoke unto you, saying, You *are* spies:
15   Hereby you shall be proved: By the life of Pharaoh you shall not go forth hence, except your youngest brother come hither.
16   Send one of you, and let him fetch your brother, and you shall be kept in prison, that your words may be proved, whether *there be any* truth in you: or else by the life of Pharaoh surely you *are* spies.
17   And he put them all together into ward three days.
18   And Joseph said unto them the third day, This do, and live; *for* I fear God:
19   If you *be* true *men*, let one of your brethren be bound in the house of your prison: go you, carry corn for the famine of your houses:
20   But bring your youngest brother unto me; so shall your words be verified, and you shall not die. And they did so.

At bare minimum, it has been at least twenty years since Joseph has seen his family. We know Joseph's age was thirty when he was standing before Pharaoh. The seven years of plenty have passed and the famine has effected even the lands northward into Caanan. These ten brothers that came to Egypt, did so with a sense of urgency to provide for their families. The very brothers who sold him into slavery after putting him in a pit. Joseph was very aware of who was missing! Where was Benjamin, his baby brother?! Had they killed him or sold him into slavery also? Yes, they told him they left him at home. But could he trust that claim from men who sold their own brother into slavery?

Joseph is proclaiming here that he is his brother's keeper if he is still alive. Joseph is saying Cain got it wrong. YES! YOU ARE YOUR BROTHER'S Keeper!

Dear Lord Jesus,

Joseph worked hard in preparing for this time of famine. You used this time of tragedy to reunite a family. Lord, You love us so much You give us time to forget our sorrows, time to lessen our anger, and even better, time to come to a place of forgiveness. Lord, please continue to work on me to be the person You want!

In Jesus name, Amen.

DAY #111
GENESIS 42:21-38

21   And they said one to another, We *are* verily guilty concerning our brother, in that we saw the anguish of his soul, when he besought us, and we would not hear; therefore is this distress come upon us.

22   And Reuben answered them, saying, Spoke I not unto you, saying, Do not sin against the child; and you would not hear? therefore, behold, also his blood is required.

23 And they knew not that Joseph understood *them*; for he spoke unto them by an interpreter.

24 And he turned himself about from them, and wept; and returned to them again, and communed with them, and took from them Simeon, and bound him before their eyes.

25 Then Joseph commanded to fill their sacks with corn, and to restore every man's money into his sack, and to give them provision for the way: and thus did he unto them.

26 And they loaded their asses with the corn, and departed from there.

27 And as one of them opened his sack to give his ass provender in the inn, he espied his money; for, behold, it *was* in his sack's mouth.

28 And he said unto his brethren, My money is restored; and, lo, *it is* even in my sack: and their heart failed *them*, and they were afraid, saying one to another, What *is* this *that* God has done unto us?

29 And they came unto Jacob their father unto the land of Canaan, and told him all that befell unto them; saying,

30 The man, *who is* the lord of the land, spoke roughly to us, and took us for spies of the country.

31 And we said unto him, We *are* true *men*; we are no spies:

32 We *be* twelve brethren, sons of our father; one *is* not, and the youngest *is* this day with our father in the land of Canaan.

33 And the man, the lord of the country, said unto us, Hereby shall I know that you *are* true *men*; leave one of your brethren *here* with me, and take *food for* the famine of your households, and be gone:

34 And bring your youngest brother unto me: then shall I know that you *are* not spies, but *that* you *are* true *men: so* will I deliver you your brother, and you shall traffick in the land.

35 And it came to pass as they emptied their sacks, that, behold, every man's bundle of money *was* in his sack: and

when *both* they and their father saw the bundles of money, they were afraid.

36   And Jacob their father said unto them, Me have you bereaved *of my children*: Joseph *is* not, and Simeon *is* not, and you will take Benjamin *away*: all these things are against me.

37   And Reuben spoke unto his father, saying, Slay my two sons, if I bring him not to you: deliver him into my hand, and I will bring him to you again.

38   And he said, My son shall not go down with you; for his brother is dead, and he is left alone: if mischief befall him by the way in the which you go, then shall you bring down my gray hairs with sorrow to the grave.

Put yourself in the shoes of Joseph's brothers. You have taken part in the sale of one of your brothers. You get put in prison for just doing what everyone else was doing, buying food to bring home. You get accused of being spies and swear honestly that you are not. But you get put into prison. You and each of your brothers have children and they have children now. You have servants, sheep, and more. Their very survival depends on your successful return of the food you came to buy. Yet, here you are in prison. The man who put you in prison returns and offers you an out. Leave one of your brothers behind, and go home. That brother will be freed if you just bring your baby brother and show him to that man. You leave your brother behind and hurriedly rush home because of the great need for this food. All the time you are rehearsing in your head how you will explain this to your father. When you finally do explain it you discover every brother including yourself has returned with every last coin you brought to buy the food. Before you were accused of being spies. NOW YOU ARE A THIEF! How quickly would you return?

How willing would you be to race down and save one brother possibly costing your own lives? Would you be willing to step forward to save your own brother/sister knowing you could die? This was the situation. The nine brothers saw it and Israel, their father saw it. Simeon the brother left behind had to be thinking after they didn't return in a timely manner, that they sold him off just like they had their brother Joseph. He had no idea what Joseph had set into motion.

How would you have acted if you were one of Joseph's older brothers?

Dear Lord Jesus,

Thank you for being my strong tower. You deliver me from fear. I can face the unknown, the scary, and even death because You are here for me. You love even me, so I can do this! Without You – I would not be able to face much and fear would overrun my person. Lord, Thank you, for Your great love!

In Jesus name, Amen.

DAY #112
GENESIS 43:1-15

1 And the famine *was* sore in the land.
2 And it came to pass, when they had eaten up the corn which they had brought out of Egypt, their father said unto them, Go again, buy us a little food.
3 And Judah spoke unto him, saying, The man did solemnly protest unto us, saying, You shall not see my face, except your brother *be* with you.
4 If you *will* send our brother with us, we will go down and buy you food:
5 But if you *will* not send *him*, we will not go down: for the man said unto us, You shall not see my face, except your brother *be* with you.
6 And Israel said, Why dealt you *so* ill with me, *as* to tell the man whether you had yet a brother?
7 And they said, The man asked us straitly of our state, and of our kindred, saying, *is* your father yet alive? have you *another* brother? and we told him according to the tenor of these words: could we certainly know that he would say, Bring your brother down?
8 And Judah said unto Israel his father, Send the lad with me, and we will arise and go; that we may live, and not die, both we, and you, *and* also our little ones.
9 I will be surety for him; of my hand shall you require him: if I bring him not unto you, and set him before you, then let me bear the blame for ever:
10 For except we had lingered, surely now we had returned this second time.
11 And their father Israel said unto them, If *it must be* so now, do this; take of the best fruits in the land in your vessels,

	and carry down the man a present, a little balm, and a little honey, spices, and myrrh, nuts, and almonds:
12	And take double money in your hand; and the money that was brought again in the mouth of your sacks, carry *it* again in your hand; peradventure it *was* an oversight:
13	Take also your brother, and arise, go again unto the man:
14	And God Almighty give you mercy before the man, that he may send away your other brother, and Benjamin. If I be bereaved *of my children*, I am bereaved.
15	And the men took that present, and they took double money in their hand, and Benjamin; and rose up, and went down to Egypt, and stood before Joseph.

How long did Israel wait before he asked his sons to return to Egypt?

Put yourself in his shoes. What would it take for you to send your own children to a place where they could be killed after having been set up to appear as thieves during a famine? Last time they went and came back minus one brother. Now Israel had lost two sons…. Worse, the one child that stayed behind at home last time, is the one the man in Egypt wants to see. The baby though now grown has to go or you can't get any food, and still, there is a risk that all eleven may be killed by the man in Egypt. But if they do not go … it is likely you will all die.

This is what J. Vernon McGee describes as one of the most dramatic moments in the entire Bible. The fear of sacrificing your children if you send them more food vs. the inevitability of dying of hunger if they do not go. You send them. No, all you can do is sit and wait unsure of what will happen next.

Dear Lord Jesus,

Sometimes even when I think I do what is right I agonize over the choice I made. Was it right or wrong, bounces around in my head. Lord, I know you are there with me as I fight my own sinful nature. Lord, help me to stand stronger each day on Your Word. Help me to trust that You are in charge and know what You are doing. Lord, thank you!

In Jesus name, Amen.

DAY #113
GENESIS 43:16-34

16   And when Joseph saw Benjamin with them, he said to the ruler of his house, Bring *these* men home, and slay, and make ready; for *these* men shall dine with me at noon.
17   And the man did as Joseph bade; and the man brought the men into Joseph's house.
18   And the men were afraid, because they were brought into Joseph's house; and they said, Because of the money that was returned in our sacks at the first time are we brought in; that he may seek occasion against us, and fall upon us, and take us for bondmen, and our asses.
19   And they came near to the steward of Joseph's house, and they communed with him at the door of the house,
20   And said, O sir, we came indeed down at the first time to buy food:
21   And it came to pass, when we came to the inn, that we opened our sacks, and, behold, *every* man's money *was* in

the mouth of his sack, our money in full weight: and we have brought it again in our hand.

22 And other money have we brought down in our hands to buy food: we cannot tell who put our money in our sacks.

23 And he said, Peace *be* to you, fear not: your God, and the God of your father, ha given you treasure in your sacks: I had your money. And he brought Simeon out unto them.

24 And the man brought the men into Joseph's house, and gave *them* water, and they washed their feet; and he gave their asses provender.

25 And they made ready the present against Joseph came at noon: for they heard that they should eat bread there.

26 And when Joseph came home, they brought him the present which *was* in their hand into the house, and bowed themselves to him to the earth.

27 And he asked them of *their* welfare, and said, *is* your father well, the old man of whom you spoke? *is* he yet alive?

28 And they answered, Your servant our father *is* in good health, he *is* yet alive. And they bowed down their heads, and made obeisance.

29 And he lifted up his eyes, and saw his brother Benjamin, his mother's son, and said, *is* this your younger brother, of whom you spoke unto me? And he said, God be gracious unto you, my son.

30 And Joseph made haste; for his bowels did yearn upon his brother: and he sought *a place* to weep; and he entered into *his* chamber, and wept there.

31 And he washed his face, and went out, and refrained himself, and said, Set on bread.

32 And they set on for him by himself, and for them by themselves, and for the Egyptians, which did eat with him, by themselves: because the Egyptians might not eat bread with the Hebrews; for that *is* an abomination unto the Egyptians.

33 And they sat before him, the firstborn according to his birthright, and the youngest according to his youth: and the men marveled one at another.
34 And he took *and sent* plates of food unto them from before him: but Benjamin's plate of food was five times any of theirs. And they drank, and were merry with him.

Note that Joseph's brothers hide nothing. They returned and disclosed everything about their money being returned to them. They do not wait for an appropriate moment to reveal this, they tell Joseph's steward. In doing this, each of them at this point is now thinking that they returning with an unexpected financial gain. On top of this, there is something else distinct that should have caught their ears. The one who they told, Responded to them speaking of God blessing them. This should have seemed a little strange to them given that so many people groups of their time spoke of gods and not one God.

Joseph enters and his brothers minus Benjamin approach. He asks about their father first, then they introduce their brother Benjamin. Joseph's closest brother. The one he had watched over and helped care for now before him as a young man. His eyes roamed over Joseph remembering the baby he knew. Seeing those features carved into the man before him today. It was too much. The emotion of the moment forced him out of the "high and mighty role" he played, into a man weeping in joy. Joseph knows now, is the time!

Joseph was second to the pharaoh and no one else. He was as close to the top as possible, and yet the Egyptians outside his wife and children would not eat with him. It's the opposite to nomadic customs, where all visitors are provided some hospitality with food and water. Joseph uses this moment to be the servant-leader and reveal himself step by step. He sets the places. His brothers marvel that he got their birth order perfectly. Then when Joseph serves them, he gives Benjamin 5 times the amount as the others. No one complains, like jealous children! These are men. Men who know their own sins. They are grateful for what they receive. "They drank and were merry with him," but still did not know this man of authority in front of them was their own brother Joseph.

Dear Lord Jesus,

When others are blessed by You. Let me take great joy in celebrating that blessing. Let me see that as Your love in action! Lord, I want Your blessings, but I should never be jealous of what others have. Like Joseph's brothers this day, let me be merry in celebration with those who are blessed! Lord, I want to grow more in You. I want to be a person who is known not for myself, but for what YOU have done in me. Lord, may You be blessed in all that I do.

In Jesus name, Amen.

DAY #114
GENESIS 44:1-34

1   And he commanded the steward of his house, saying, Fill the men's sacks *with* food, as much as they can carry, and put every man's money in his sack's mouth.

2   And put my cup, the silver cup, in the sack's mouth of the youngest, and his corn money. And he did according to the word that Joseph had spoken.

3   As soon as the morning was light, the men were sent away, they and their asses.

4   *And* when they were gone out of the city, *and* not *yet* far off, Joseph said unto his steward, Up, follow after the men; and when you do overtake them, say unto them, Why have you rewarded evil for good?

5   *Is* not this *from* which my lord drinks, and whereby indeed he divines? You have done evil in so doing.

6   And he overtook them, and he spoke unto them these same words.

7   And they said unto him, Why says my lord these words? God forbid that your servants should do according to this thing:

8   Behold, the money, which we found in our sacks' mouths, we brought again unto you out of the land of Canaan: how then should we steal out of your lord's house silver or gold?

9   With whomsoever of your servants it be found, both let him die, and we also will be my lord's bondmen.

10   And he said, Now also *let* it *be* according unto your words: he with whom it is found shall be my servant; and you shall be blameless.

11   Then they speedily took down every man his sack to the ground, and opened every man his sack.

12   And he searched, *and* began at the eldest, and left at the youngest: and the cup was found in Benjamin's sack.

13   Then they rent their clothes, and laded every man his ass, and returned to the city.

14   And Judah and his brethren came to Joseph's house; for he *was* yet there: and they fell before him on the ground.

15   And Joseph said unto them, What deed *is* this that you have done? wot you not that such a man as I can certainly divine?
16   And Judah said, What shall we say unto my lord? what shall we speak? or how shall we clear ourselves? God has found out the iniquity of your servants: behold, we *are* my lord's servants, both we, and *he* also with whom the cup is found.
17   And he said, God forbid that I should do so: *but* the man in whose hand the cup is found, he shall be my servant; and as for you, get you up in peace unto your father.
18   Then Judah came near unto him, and said, Oh my lord, let your servant, I pray you, speak a word in my lord's ears, and let not your anger burn against your servant: for you *are* even as Pharaoh.
19   My lord asked his servants, saying, Have you a father, or a brother?
20   And we said unto my lord, We have a father, an old man, and a child of his old age, a little one; and his brother is dead, and he alone is left of his mother, and his father loveth him.
21   And you said unto your servants, Bring him down unto me, that I may set mine eyes upon him.
22   And we said unto my lord, The lad cannot leave his father: for *if* he should leave his father, *his father* would die.
23   And you said unto your servants, Except your youngest brother come down with you, you shall see my face no more.
24   And it came to pass when we came up unto your servant my father, we told him the words of my lord.
25   And our father said, Go again, *and* buy us a little food.
26   And we said, We cannot go down: if our youngest brother be with us, then will we go down: for we may not see the man's face, except our youngest brother *be* with us.

27 And your servant my father said unto us, You know that my wife bare me two *sons*:
28 And the one went out from me, and I said, Surely he is torn in pieces; and I saw him not since:
29 And if you take this also from me, and mischief befall him, you shall bring down my gray hairs with sorrow to the grave.
30 Now therefore when I come to your servant my father, and the lad *be* not with us; seeing that his life is bound up in the lad's life;
31 It shall come to pass, when he sees that the lad *is* not *with us*, that he will die: and your servants shall bring down the gray hairs of your servant our father with sorrow to the grave.
32 For your servant became surety for the lad unto my father, saying, If I bring him not unto you, then I shall bear the blame to my father forever.
33 Now therefore, I pray you, let your servant abide instead of the lad a bondman to my lord; and let the lad go up with his brethren.
34 For how shall I go up to my father, and the lad *be* not with me? lest peradventure I see the evil that shall come on my father.

A trap set and sprung perfectly. That is what this chapter is all about. Joseph sets the trap to see if his brothers still continue with evil in their hearts. Benjamin would be the favored child now. Would they easily let him "disappear" as they did Joseph, or would they sacrifice to prevent it?

Joseph wanted to know if his brothers still had evil intentions in their hearts. He wanted to know if jealousy still led them about and motivated them. Judah's unending impassioned plea for Benjamin was the answer Joseph was hoping for.

Thirteen years passed before Joseph stood before Pharaoh. Another seven passed before the famine was upon them. It was now the second year of the famine for the second trip of the children of Israel. Twenty-two years had passed. If the other sons of Israel had so bound themselves to the sin of jealousy, Joseph had to know so he could protect Benjamin and their father.

Dear Lord Jesus,

I thank you for the blessings you have given me and continue to grant me. Lord, remove whatever stumbling blocks are in my path so that I may continue to change and grow in You more each day. You have taken me, and molded me into a much better person, step by step with great patience on Your end. Lord, please do not stop this work you are doing in me.

In Jesus name, Amen.

DAY #115
GENESIS 45:1-24

1   Then Joseph could not refrain himself before all them that stood by him; and he cried, Cause every man to go out from me. And there stood no man with him, while Joseph made himself known unto his brethren.

2   And he wept aloud: and the Egyptians and the house of Pharaoh heard.
3   And Joseph said unto his brethren, I *am* Joseph; does my father yet live? And his brethren could not answer him; for they were troubled at his presence.
4   And Joseph said unto his brethren, Come near to me, I pray you. And they came near. And he said, I *am* Joseph your brother, whom you sold into Egypt.
5   Now therefore be not grieved, nor angry with yourselves, that you sold me here: for God did send me before you to preserve life.
6   For these two years *has* the famine *been* in the land: and yet *there are* five years, in the which *there shall* neither *be* earing nor harvest.
7   And God sent me before you to preserve you a posterity in the earth, and to save your lives by a great deliverance.
8   So now *it was* not you *that* sent me here, but God: and he has made me a father to Pharaoh, and lord of all his house, and a ruler throughout all the land of Egypt.
9   Haste you, and go up to my father, and say unto him, Thus says your son Joseph, God has made me lord of all Egypt: come down unto me, tarry not:
10 And you shall dwell in the land of Goshen, and you shall be near unto me, you, and your children, and your children's children, and your flocks, and your herds, and all that you have:
11 And there will I nourish you; for yet *there are* five years of famine; lest you, and your household, and all that you have, come to poverty.
12 And, behold, your eyes see, and the eyes of my brother Benjamin, that *it is* my mouth that speaks unto you.

13 And you shall tell my father of all my glory in Egypt, and of all that you have seen; and you shall haste and bring down my father hither.

14 And he fell upon his brother Benjamin's neck, and wept; and Benjamin wept upon his neck.

15 Moreover he kissed all his brethren, and wept upon them: and after that his brethren talked with him.

16 And the fame thereof was heard in Pharaoh's house, saying, Joseph's brethren are come: and it pleased Pharaoh well, and his servants.

17 And Pharaoh said unto Joseph, Say unto your brethren, This do you; lade your beasts, and go, get you unto the land of Canaan;

18 And take your father and your households, and come unto me: and I will give you the good of the land of Egypt, and you shall eat the fat of the land.

19 Now you art commanded, this do you; take you wagons out of the land of Egypt for your little ones, and for your wives, and bring your father, and come.

20 Also regard not your stuff; for the good of all the land of Egypt *is* yours.

21 And the children of Israel did so: and Joseph gave them wagons, according to the commandment of Pharaoh, and gave them provision for the way.

22 To all of them he gave each man changes of raiment; but to Benjamin he gave three hundred *pieces* of silver, and five changes of raiment.

23 And to his father he sent after this *manner*; ten asses laden with the good things of Egypt, and ten she asses laden with corn and bread and meat for his father by the way.

24 So he sent his brethren away, and they departed: and he said unto them, See that you fall not out by the way.

Joseph had lost all of his "dignified" composure and cried as he revealed that he indeed was their brother. The ten brothers listening have to be experiencing so many emotions. Fear, relief, shock, joy, and wonder would be constantly coursing through them. The fear of being found out is now gone. Their sin was revealed and the fear of being found as such a scum that would sell his own brother is gone. Joseph puts all their fear at ease. He understands he is God's man at this appointed time only because his brothers, as mean and jealous as they were at the time, were doing something that had to be done, to put him in the place he needed to be to help both Egypt and them.

For most men, this would be a scary unveiling. But Joseph's acknowledgement that God put him where he is to save them all was somehow so honest, and straightforward, they felt no fear in his presence. They hear Joseph's request for them to come live with him through the famine.

The joyous acknowledgement of his family is shared quickly by the servants to Pharaoh and all of Egypt. Pharaoh commands them to use his wagons to bring their entire family and all they possess to Egypt, with a promise of blessings to come.

His brothers happily return, somehow they know that even when their father knows the evil they did end up being a blessing to him, he will rejoice with them at their brother's reappearance. This says something about how the brothers acknowledge their father differently. Before they were jealous. They are protective at this time and only care that he is happy.

These same men, Joseph's ten older brothers, have one additional task. One that no one wants, ever. They have to expose their sin to their wives and children. This was a heavy burden for their journey home. But revealing this would also come with the sharing that GOD used this to save them all!

Parents are supposed to direct their children's instruction and obedience, but revealing their own imperfections and sins is also something we must do so, our children can see us not as perfect, but as imperfect men and women whom God uses.

Dear Lord Jesus,

Lord help me to be one who is able to admit my own faults and sins. Let me not hide them, but seek to confess them before you first! Lord, who am I but a sinner You love. Help me to hide my sins from anyone. Give me the ability to own up to them. Give me the ability to beg forgiveness from those whom I have sinned against.

In Jesus name, Amen.

DAY #116
GENESIS 45:25-28

25 And they went up out of Egypt, and came into the land of Canaan unto Jacob their father,
26 And told him, saying, Joseph *is* yet alive, and he *is* governor over all the land of Egypt. And Jacob's heart fainted, for he believed them not.
27 And they told him all the words of Joseph, which he had said unto them: and when he saw the wagons which Joseph had sent to carry him, the spirit of Jacob their father revived:

28   And Israel said, *it is* enough; Joseph my son *is* yet alive: I will go and see him before I die.

Can you imagine what it would have taken if your own children came to you telling you a child you believed was dead and unheard of for over twenty years was suddenly found and not only alive but one of the most influential men alive? Would you believe your children? Today we might want proof, a teleconference, a video chat, or something! What they had was wagons.

Now there would be a sense of urgency! Israel could probably be seen racing about giving instructions to break camp and prepare for the move. He could probably have been heard yelling joyously that his son, Joseph is alive, make ready and prepare to go see him!

When you're excited about something you can't shut up! You want to share it over and over!

Dear Lord Jesus!

You are the great and living GOD! You make the impossible possible. You give me reasons each day to sing Your praises! Lord, how is it the world can seem dreary or boring when you do so much just for me! Lord God, let me see more of Your wonders!

In Jesus name, Amen.

DAY #117
GENESIS 46:1-4

1   And Israel took his journey with all that he had, and came to Beersheba, and offered sacrifices unto the God of his father Isaac.
2   And God spoke unto Israel in the visions of the night, and said, Jacob, Jacob. And he said, Here *am* I.
3   And he said, I *am* God, the God of your father: fear not to go down into Egypt; for I will there make of you a great nation:
4   I will go down with you into Egypt; and I will also surely bring you up *again*: and Joseph shall put his hand upon your eyes.

Why did Joseph stop in Beersheba? It is because Beersheba was an important place in the faith of his father, his grandfather, and himself. God had promised this land to him, not Egypt. Abraham and Abimelech made a pact there. Abraham dwelt there having dug wells and planted a grove of trees (Gen 21). Isaac Jacob's father spent time there with his father, and also met God there (Gen 26:24). It was an important place not only to him personally as something he had called home, but to his faith. What better a place to call on God, and make sure of what he was about to do as something he should do not something he wants to do because of his heart so wanting to see his son Joseph?

God does not disappoint Israel. He meets him there! He sends Jacob on into Egypt with all that he has with him, with a great blessing, of making Israel into a great nation while they are in Egypt.

God is good at bringing us out of our comfort zones. Sometimes we have a stubborn desire to enjoy where we are more than where God is leading us. When God wants us to move on, we get on nervous dig in our heels, and try to slow the process. Checking with God is not slowing the process. It is part of the process. Israel trusted and then verified. He acted then double-checked with God to make sure what he was about to do was not wrong. What a great Father! What a true man of God Israel had become! The blessing he receives for checking with God that day is still evident and nothing any man can deny. Israel is indeed a nation!

Dear Lord Jesus,

You call us from that which is comfortable to that which seems prickly as we look on. We are Yours, yet choosing to follow You gave us no promise of an easy day. You told of persecution and hatred against us and more. Lord, use me! Put me where You want me. Teach me more and more, so that I may become the person You want me to be!

In Jesus name, Amen.

DAY #118
GENESIS 46:5-34

5   And Jacob rose up from Beersheba: and the sons of Israel carried Jacob their father, and their little ones, and their wives, in the wagons which Pharaoh had sent to carry him.
6   And they took their cattle, and their goods, which they had gotten in the land of Canaan, and came into Egypt, Jacob, and all his seed with him:

7   His sons, and his sons' sons with him, his daughters, and his sons' daughters, and all his seed brought he with him into Egypt.

8   And these *are* the names of the children of Israel, which came into Egypt, Jacob and his sons: Reuben, Jacob's firstborn.

9   And the sons of Reuben; Hanoch, and Phallu, and Hezron, and Carmi.

10   And the sons of Simeon; Jemuel, and Jamin, and Ohad, and Jachin, and Zohar, and Shaul the son of a Canaanitish woman.

11   And the sons of Levi; Gershon, Kohath, and Merari.

12   And the sons of Judah; Er, and Onan, and Shelah, and Pharez, and Zerah: but Er and Onan died in the land of Canaan. And the sons of Pharez were Hezron and Hamul.

13   And the sons of Issachar; Tola, and Phuvah, and Job, and Shimron.

14   And the sons of Zebulun; Sered, and Elon, and Jahleel.

15   These *be* the sons of Leah, which she bare unto Jacob in Padanaram, with his daughter Dinah: all the souls of his sons and his daughters *were* thirty and three.

16   And the sons of Gad; Ziphion, and Haggi, Shuni, and Ezbon, Eri, and Arodi, and Areli.

17   And the sons of Asher; Jimnah, and Ishuah, and Isui, and Beriah, and Serah their sister: and the sons of Beriah; Heber, and Malchiel.

18   These *are* the sons of Zilpah, whom Laban gave to Leah his daughter, and these she bare unto Jacob, *even* sixteen souls.

19   The sons of Rachel Jacob's wife; Joseph, and Benjamin.

20   And unto Joseph in the land of Egypt were born Manasseh and Ephraim, which Asenath the daughter of Potipherah priest of On bare unto him.

21 And the sons of Benjamin *were* Belah, and Becher, and Ashbel, Gera, and Naaman, Ehi, and Rosh, Muppim, and Huppim, and Ard.

22 These *are* the sons of Rachel, which were born to Jacob: all the souls *were* fourteen.

23 And the sons of Dan; Hushim.

24 And the sons of Naphtali; Jahzeel, and Guni, and Jezer, and Shillem.

25 These *are* the sons of Bilhah, which Laban gave unto Rachel his daughter, and she bare these unto Jacob: all the souls *were* seven.

26 All the souls that came with Jacob into Egypt, which came out of his loins, besides Jacob's sons' wives, all the souls *were* threescore and six;

27 And the sons of Joseph, which were born him in Egypt, *were* two souls: all the souls of the house of Jacob, which came into Egypt, *were* threescore and ten.

28 And he sent Judah before him unto Joseph, to direct his face unto Goshen; and they came into the land of Goshen.

29 And Joseph made ready his chariot, and went up to meet Israel his father, to Goshen, and presented himself unto him; and he fell on his neck, and wept on his neck a good while.

30 And Israel said unto Joseph, Now let me die, since I have seen your face, because you *are* yet alive.

31 And Joseph said unto his brethren, and unto his father's house, I will go up, and shew Pharaoh, and say unto him, My brethren, and my father's house, which *were* in the land of Canaan, are come unto me;

32 And the men *are* shepherds, for their trade has been to feed cattle; and they have brought their flocks, and their herds, and all that they have.

33   And it shall come to pass, when Pharaoh shall call you, and shall say, What *is* your occupation?

34   That you shall say, Your servants' trade has been about cattle from our youth even until now, both we, *and* also our fathers: that you may dwell in the land of Goshen; for every shepherd *is* an abomination unto the Egyptians.

Israel and all that is his comes to Egypt's land of Goshen. Excluding the wives, they are seventy in all including Joseph and his children. Joseph and his father are finally united in a tear-filled heartfelt meeting. He calls his brothers and father together and tells them how their first interaction has to go and he asks them to tell Pharaoh what we would describe as a white lie. This tells u a little about Joseph who rose from the status of a slave convict to the one in charge of Egypt. Joseph here may not know it, but he is telling of things to come.

Dear Lord Jesus,

You are the God who does impossible things! You provided a way for a country to not only have enough through a seven-year drought, It also saved Israel. Lord, help me to keep my eyes open to what is happening around me. Help me to watch and be wary. Use me, Lord, to not only share truth with the lost but to be one who helps others grow in You.

In Jesus name, Amen.

DAY #119
GENESIS 47:1-10

1 Then Joseph came and told Pharaoh, and said, My father and my brethren, and their flocks, and their herds, and all that they have, are come out of the land of Canaan; and, behold, they *are* in the land of Goshen.
2 And he took some of his brethren, *even* five men, and presented them unto Pharaoh.
3 And Pharaoh said unto his brethren, What *is* your occupation? And they said unto Pharaoh, Your servants *are* shepherds, both we, *and* also our fathers.
4 They said moreover unto Pharaoh, For to sojourn in the land are we come; for your servants have no pasture for their flocks; for the famine *is* sore in the land of Canaan: now therefore, we pray you, let your servants dwell in the land of Goshen.
5 And Pharaoh spoke unto Joseph, saying, Your father and your brethren are come unto you:
6 The land of Egypt *is* before you; in the best of the land make your father and brethren to dwell; in the land of Goshen let them dwell: and if you know *any* men of activity among them, then make them rulers over my cattle.
7 And Joseph brought in Jacob his father, and set him before Pharaoh: and Jacob blessed Pharaoh.
8 And Pharaoh said unto Jacob, How old *are* you?
9 And Jacob said unto Pharaoh, The days of the years of my pilgrimage *are* an hundred and thirty years: few and evil have the days of the years of my life been, and have not

       attained unto the days of the years of the life of my fathers in the days of their pilgrimage.

10   And Jacob blessed Pharaoh, and went out from before Pharaoh.

If you were Pharaoh and had this horrible dream that ended up predicting the famine that you were now experiencing, and the interpreter of it, that you chose to rule over the land as your second in command now makes YOU LOOK GREAT AND WISE, would you bless or curse that person's family as they came?

Pharaoh saw this as an opportunity to say thank you to God's chosen person to handle this famine, Joseph. He also had to be extremely curious about Joseph's handling of his brothers. Now, he has the chance to meet his father! His mind had to be pondering how wise this man, whose son, had so blessed Egypt. He orders Joseph to place his brethren in positions of power if he trusts their ability. He also orders a blessing upon why there shall live. This removes any doubt by any Egyptian noble, or royal as to the right of Joseph's family to be placed in Goshen and to attain positions of power.

Jacob arrives in Egypt when he is 130 years old. He probably saw a need to thank Pharaoh for the opportunity to reunite with his son Joseph. But, Jacob knew this was all God's doing, still he wanted to do something, something only he could do for Pharaoh in return. He blessed Pharaoh.

Dear Lord Jesus,

Lord, you deserve my praise and thanks for all you do! Lord, please allow me to be used by You as thanks and praise for you're the work you have done and continue to do within me. You took me, a wretched sinner, and made me into who I am today. Use me, Lord.

In Jesus name, Amen.

DAY #120
GENESIS 47:11-27

11   And Joseph placed his father and his brethren, and gave them a possession in the land of Egypt, in the best of the land, in the land of Rameses, as Pharaoh had commanded.
12   And Joseph nourished his father, and his brethren, and all his father's household, with bread, according to *their* families.
13   And *there was* no bread in all the land; for the famine *was* very sore, so that the land of Egypt and *all* the land of Canaan fainted by reason of the famine.
14   And Joseph gathered up all the money that was found in the land of Egypt, and in the land of Canaan, for the corn which they bought: and Joseph brought the money into Pharaoh's house.
15   And when money failed in the land of Egypt, and in the land of Canaan, all the Egyptians came unto Joseph, and said, Give us bread: for why should we die in your presence? for the money fails.
16   And Joseph said, Give your cattle; and I will give you for your cattle, if money fail.
17   And they brought their cattle unto Joseph: and Joseph gave them bread *in exchange* for horses, and for the flocks, and

for the cattle of the herds, and for the asses: and he fed them with bread for all their cattle for that year.

18 When that year was ended, they came unto him the second year, and said unto him, We will not hide *it* from my lord, how that our money is spent; my lord also has our herds of cattle; there is not ought left in the sight of my lord, but our bodies, and our lands:

19 Why shall we die before your eyes, both we and our land? buy us and our land for bread, and we and our land will be servants unto Pharaoh: and give *us* seed, that we may live, and not die, that the land be not desolate.

20 And Joseph bought all the land of Egypt for Pharaoh; for the Egyptians sold every man his field, because the famine prevailed over them: so the land became Pharaoh's.

21 And as for the people, he removed them to cities from *one* end of the borders of Egypt even to the *other* end thereof.

22 Only the land of the priests bought he not; for the priests had a portion *assigned them* of Pharaoh, and did eat their portion which Pharaoh gave them: why they sold not their lands.

23 Then Joseph said unto the people, Behold, I have bought you this day and your land for Pharaoh: lo, *here is* seed for you, and you shall sow the land.

24 And it shall come to pass in the increase, that you shall give the fifth *part* unto Pharaoh, and four parts shall be your own, for seed of the field, and for your food, and for them of your households, and for food for your little ones.

25 And they said, You have saved our lives: let us find grace in the sight of my lord, and we will be Pharaoh's servants.

26 And Joseph made it a law over the land of Egypt unto this day, *that* Pharaoh should have the fifth *part*; except the land of the priests only, *which* became not Pharaoh's.

27   And Israel dwelt in the land of Egypt, in the country of Goshen; and they had possessions therein, and grew, and multiplied exceedingly.

Egypt lived through this famine of years because of what Joseph had done. The people saw that the wisdom of Pharaoh's administrator got them through this. They sold off all they had with the exception of selling themselves. Now they owed Pharaoh. The famine ended and Joseph had prepared for that moment as well. He called those who had sold off their land and returned it to them telling them to give Pharaoh 20 percent. It is not said if this meant in crops or of the profit made. The joy of being handed back the land you owed by giving 20 percent must have catapulted the favor of Pharaoh to his people even higher.

Note that verse 27 says that Israel did not suffer equally. They kept their possessions and multiplied. This is indeed of interest. Remember they came with their flocks and herds. It is only with God's blessings this would be possible. This had to be noticeable by the people and pharaoh. The Egyptians would have noticed that Joseph's family was working and helping administer the distribution of food and more. Yet, it seems they were not complained against but accepted as co-laborers.

Dear Lord Jesus,

The wisdom of Joseph was credited to You by him. He gives You the glory! Lord open my eyes that I too may see more is seen by the average person. I want to give You the glory for what I see that others do not. But more so, I want to be able to see what You see when I feel blind to what is happening. Lord, use me so others may see Your love.

In Jesus name, Amen.

DAY #121
GENESIS 47:28-31

28   And Jacob lived in the land of Egypt seventeen years: so the whole age of Jacob was an hundred forty and seven years.
29   And the time drew nigh that Israel must die: and he called his son Joseph, and said unto him, If now I have found grace in your sight, put, I pray you, your hand under my thigh, and deal kindly and truly with me; bury me not, I pray you, in Egypt:
30   But I will lie with my fathers, and you shall carry me out of Egypt, and bury me in their burying place. And he said, I will do as you have said.
31   And he said, Swear unto me. And he sware unto him. And Israel bowed himself upon the bed's head.

At the age of 147, Israel is facing his departure from this earth. He has been seventeen years in the land of Egypt. He probably thought that as soon as the famine ended they would return to Canaan. But it was not yet God's timing. There was such faith in Israel, that this time would come, that he committed the promise to return his remains to the land promised to him by God. There was something about that promised land that compelled even on the edge of death to have his remains returned to it. This was not a superstition, but a promise received from God that was fully believed!

Dear Lord Jesus,

You never cease to amaze us. You offer us life through Your offering of Your own person in our place. You make promises and keep them even though we are so undeserving of any one of them. Lord, guide my steps. Help me to step out in faith and become the person You desire. Lead me in the direction You desire.

In Jesus name, Amen.

DAY #123
GENESIS 48:1-7

1 And it came to pass after these things, that *one* told Joseph, Behold, your father *is* sick: and he took with him his two sons, Manasseh and Ephraim.
2 And *one* told Jacob, and said, Behold, your son Joseph comes unto you: and Israel strengthened himself, and sat upon the bed.
3 And Jacob said unto Joseph, God Almighty appeared unto me at Luz in the land of Canaan, and blessed me,
4 And said unto me, Behold, I will make you fruitful, and multiply you, and I will make of you a multitude of people;

	and will give this land to your seed after you *for* an everlasting possession.
5	And now your two sons, Ephraim and Manasseh, which were born unto you in the land of Egypt before I came unto you into Egypt, *are* mine; as Reuben and Simeon, they shall be mine.
6	And your issue, which you begettest after them, shall be your, *and* shall be called after the name of their brethren in their inheritance.
7	And as for me, when I came from Padan, Rachel died by me in the land of Canaan in the way, when yet *there was* but a little way to come unto Ephrath: and I buried her there in the way of Ephrath; the same *is* Bethlehem.

Jacob (Israel) prophecies about the tribe of Joseph. It will not be known as the tribe of Joseph but as the half-tribes of Manasseh and Ephraim. Here on Jacob's death bed, is the reason we never hear about a tribe of Joseph. Through the rest of the Bible. Jacob accepted Joseph's two sons as his own. This says something about the closeness Jacob must have felt through his seventeen years in Egypt with his lost son Joseph and his family. This is likely because Jacob resided with Joseph and was in his care. This gives an example of caring for elderly parents. Something not all of us can do.

Some might think this blessing was favoritism. Why should these two be so accepted better than any other grandchild? It is likely that Joseph's work ethic was handed down to his own children. It was slightly different than his brother's since he had been alone and a slave. Joseph understood leading meant serving. Work meant doing your best. Passing this on to his sons meant that the three would have taken turns along with Israel's eleven other sons. This would have made them stand out. Remember, Joseph was an administrator of Egypt. His sons, probably took his turn when he had to attend to the business of Egypt. This makes Jacob very aware of those around him toward the end.

Dear Lord Jesus,

Help me to live in such a way that even my presence may cause others to feel Your love. I do not want to promote me, but You! I am but an imperfect example. I have my own struggles following You. Lord, this is why I need you to continue working on me and changing me from within.

In Jesus name, Amen.

DAY #124
GENESIS 48:8-22

8   And Israel beheld Joseph's sons, and said, Who *are* these?
9   And Joseph said unto his father, They *are* my sons, whom God has given me in this *place*. And he said, Bring them, I pray you, unto me, and I will bless them.
10 Now the eyes of Israel were dim for age, *so that* he could not see. And he brought them near unto him; and he kissed them, and embraced them.
11 And Israel said unto Joseph, I had not thought to see your face: and, lo, God has shown me also your seed.
12 And Joseph brought them out from between his knees, and he bowed himself with his face to the earth.

13 And Joseph took them both, Ephraim in his right hand toward Israel's left hand, and Manasseh in his left hand toward Israel's right hand, and brought *them* near unto him.
14 And Israel stretched out his right hand, and laid *it* upon Ephraim's head, who *was* the younger, and his left hand upon Manasseh's head, guiding his hands wittingly; for Manasseh *was* the firstborn.
15 And he blessed Joseph, and said, God, before whom my fathers Abraham and Isaac did walk, the God which fed me all my life long unto this day,
16 The Angel which redeemed me from all evil, bless the lads; and let my name be named on them, and the name of my fathers Abraham and Isaac; and let them grow into a multitude in the midst of the earth.
17 And when Joseph saw that his father laid his right hand upon the head of Ephraim, it displeased him: and he held up his father's hand, to remove it from Ephraim's head unto Manasseh's head.
18 And Joseph said unto his father, Not so, my father: for this *is* the firstborn; put your right hand upon his head.
19 And his father refused, and said, I know *it*, my son, I know *it*: he also shall become a people, and he also shall be great: but truly his younger brother shall be greater than he, and his seed shall become a multitude of nations.
20 And he blessed them that day, saying, In you shall Israel bless, saying, God make you as Ephraim and as Manasseh: and he set Ephraim before Manasseh.
21 And Israel said unto Joseph, Behold, I die: but God shall be with you, and bring you again unto the land of your fathers.
22 Moreover I have given to you one portion above your brethren, which I took out of the hand of the Amorite with my sword and with my bow.

This must have struck a memory chord with Jacob (Israel) as he gave the blessing. The younger being blessed so, but this time with no deceit initiated by the younger. Parents want the best for their children. Biblical times this also meant the eldest child got the biggest piece of the pie when you passed on. But God is no respecter of persons. He does not care what positions we think we hold. He knows what position we play in HIS plans. Too often greed and ambition push us to want more, when we should be accepting of what God has provided for us, to be where he wants us.

Joseph is doubly blessed, not only because he was faithful to God, but because no matter what happened to him, there may have been "poor me" thoughts, but they never prevailed! God saw Joseph accepted wherever God put him. Even if that meant slavery or prison.

When we are young and full of ambition, we do not think of how this event or that choice will effect the rest of our lives or even our children. We need to think like Joseph, and be ready to serve God, where ever he places us!

Dear Lord Jesus,

Open my eyes to those around me. Help me to see how I can bless others with what You have given me. My ambition should always be to seek Your will first. Lord work on me, that my life will be seen not as mine, but as a reflection of Your love.

In Jesus name, Amen.

DAY #125
GENESIS 49

1   And Jacob called unto his sons, and said, Gather yourselves together, that I may tell you *that* which shall befall you in the last days.
2   Gather yourselves together, and hear, you sons of Jacob; and listen unto Israel your father.
3   Reuben, you *are* my firstborn, my might, and the beginning of my strength, the excellency of dignity, and the excellency of power:
4   Unstable as water, you shall not excel; because you went up to your father's bed; then you defiled *it*: he went up to my couch.
5   Simeon and Levi *are* brethren; instruments of cruelty *are in* their habitations.
6   O my soul, come not you into their secret; unto their assembly, mine honour, be not you united: for in their anger they slew a man, and in their self-will they tore down a wall.
7   Cursed *be* their anger, for *it was* fierce; and their wrath, for it was cruel: I will divide them in Jacob, and scatter them in Israel.
8   Judah, you *are he* whom your brethren shall praise: your hand *shall be* in the neck of your enemies; your father's children shall bow down before you.
9   Judah *is* a lion's whelp: from the prey, my son, you art gone up: he stooped down, he couched as a lion, and as an old lion; who shall rouse him up?

10   The sceptre shall not depart from Judah, nor a lawgiver from between his feet, until Shiloh come; and unto him *shall* the gathering of the people *be*.
11   Binding his foal unto the vine, and his ass's colt unto the choice vine; he washed his garments in wine, and his clothes in the blood of grapes:
12   His eyes *shall be* red with wine, and his teeth white with milk.
13   Zebulun shall dwell at the haven of the sea; and he *shall be* for an haven of ships; and his border *shall be* unto Zidon.
14   Issachar *is* a strong ass couching down between two burdens:
15   And he saw that rest *was* good, and the land that *it was* pleasant; and bowed his shoulder to bear, and became a servant unto tribute.
16   Dan shall judge his people, as one of the tribes of Israel.
17   Dan shall be a serpent by the way, an adder in the path, that bites the horse heels, so that his rider shall fall backward.
18   I have waited for your salvation, O LORD.
19   Gad, a troop shall overcome him: but he shall overcome at the last.
20   Out of Asher his bread *shall be* fat, and he shall yield royal dainties.
21   Naphtali *is* a deer let loose: he giveth goodly words.
22   Joseph *is* a fruitful main branch, *even* a fruitful branch by a well; *whose* branches run over the wall:
23   The archers have sorely grieved him, and shot *at him*, and hated him:
24   But his bow abode in strength, and the arms of his hands were made strong by the hands of the mighty *God* of Jacob; (from there *is* the shepherd, the stone of Israel:)
25   *Even* by the God of your father, who shall help you; and by the Almighty, who shall bless you with blessings of heaven

	above, blessings of the deep that lieth under, blessings of the breasts, and of the womb:
26	The blessings of your father have prevailed above the blessings of my progenitors unto the utmost bound of the everlasting hills: they shall be on the head of Joseph, and on the crown of the head of him that was separate from his brethren.
27	Benjamin shall be as a ravenous wolf: in the morning he shall devour the prey, and at night he shall divide the spoil.
28	All these *are* the twelve tribes of Israel: and this *is it* that their father spoke unto them, and blessed them; every one according to his blessing he blessed them.
29	And he charged them, and said unto them, I am to be gathered unto my people: bury me with my fathers in the cave that *is* in the field of Ephron the Hittite,
30	In the cave that *is* in the field of Machpelah, which *is* before Mamre, in the land of Canaan, which Abraham bought with the field of Ephron the Hittite for a possession of a burying-place.
31	There they buried Abraham and Sarah his wife; there they buried Isaac and Rebekah his wife; and there I buried Leah.
32	The purchase of the field and of the cave that *is* therein *was* from the children of Heth.
33	And when Jacob had made an end of commanding his sons, he gathered up his feet into the bed, and yielded up the ghost, and was gathered unto his people.

Here we have the gathering of the children of Israel. The twelve sons are silent for fear he will die before he finishes his blessing. Death hangs in the air causing silence. The period of waiting is over. This moment is the last. They all know it.

Jacob blesses his sons and reveals their sins. This must have been harsh to listen to the raspy voice knowing its last words were NOW. The silent submissive presence of the sons having each word etched into memory. This man was their father. The man who was always there for them revealing all, blessing them in a way that was just and painful.

Dear Lord Jesus,

When death comes we lose friends and family, strangers and foes. Death brings a sense of loss. It weighs on us. Lord, thank you for being there with us. These times feel like trials, They feel like heavy burdens we must cry through. Yet, You are there listening to our every cry. Lord, let us each live better today, than we did yesterday. Let our lives impact others for You more today than yesterday. For, we are Yours!

In Jesus name, Amen.

DAY #126
GENESIS 50

1 And Joseph fell upon his father's face, and wept upon him, and kissed him.
2 And Joseph commanded his servants the physicians to embalm his father: and the physicians embalmed Israel.

3 And forty days were fulfilled for him; for so are fulfilled the days of those which are embalmed: and the Egyptians mourned for him threescore and ten days.

4 And when the days of his mourning were past, Joseph spoke unto the house of Pharaoh, saying, If now I have found grace in your eyes, speak, I pray you, in the ears of Pharaoh, saying,

5 My father made me swear, saying, Lo, I die: in my grave which I have dug for me in the land of Canaan, there shall you bury me. Now therefore let me go up, I pray you, and bury my father, and I will come again.

6 And Pharaoh said, Go up, and bury your father, according as he made you swear.

7 And Joseph went up to bury his father: and with him went up all the servants of Pharaoh, the elders of his house, and all the elders of the land of Egypt,

8 And all the house of Joseph, and his brethren, and his father's house: only their little ones, and their flocks, and their herds, they left in the land of Goshen.

9 And there went up with him both chariots and horsemen: and it was a very great company.

10 And they came to the threshing floor of Atad, which *is* beyond Jordan, and there they mourned with a great and very sore lamentation: and he made a mourning for his father seven days.

11 And when the inhabitants of the land, the Canaanites, saw the mourning in the floor of Atad, they said, This *is* a grievous mourning to the Egyptians: why the name of it was called Abelmizraim, which *is* beyond Jordan.

12 And his sons did unto him according as he commanded them:

13 For his sons carried him into the land of Canaan, and buried him in the cave of the field of Machpelah, which Abraham

bought with the field for a possession of a buryingplace of Ephron the Hittite, before Mamre.

14 And Joseph returned into Egypt, he, and his brethren, and all that went up with him to bury his father, after he had buried his father.

15 And when Joseph's brethren saw that their father was dead, they said, Joseph will peradventure hate us, and will certainly requite us all the evil which we did unto him.

16 And they sent a messenger unto Joseph, saying, Your father did command before he died, saying,

17 So shall you say unto Joseph, Forgive, I pray you now, the trespass of your brethren, and their sin; for they did unto you evil: and now, we pray you, forgive the trespass of the servants of the God of your father. And Joseph wept when they spoke unto him.

18 And his brethren also went and fell down before his face; and they said, Behold, we *be* your servants.

19 And Joseph said unto them, Fear not: for *am* I in the place of God?

20 But as for you, you thought evil against me; *but* God meant it unto good, to bring to pass, as *it is* this day, to save much people alive.

21 Now therefore fear you not: I will nourish you, and your little ones. And he comforted them, and spoke kindly unto them.

22 And Joseph dwelt in Egypt, he, and his father's house: and Joseph lived an hundred and ten years.

23 And Joseph saw Ephraim's children of the third *generation*: the children also of Machir the son of Manasseh were brought up upon Joseph's knees.

24 And Joseph said unto his brethren, I die: and God will surely visit you, and bring you out of this land unto the land which he sware to Abraham, to Isaac, and to Jacob.

25 And Joseph took an oath of the children of Israel, saying, God will surely visit you, and you shall carry up my bones from hence.
26 So Joseph died, *being* an hundred and ten years old: and they embalmed him, and he was put in a coffin in Egypt.

The mourning of Israel, who passed on from this world is finished by the preparation of his body and the burial. This would have been close to two months. The burial concludes with a return to Egypt. This return makes you wonder why only a select group came. They could have all returned to the land of their fathers. But this was not God's timing. They had grown but not to the point of becoming nations.

Joseph passes away next. His brothers' deaths are not recorded. Joseph knew they would all return one day. God must have told him of a great promise that was yet to be fulfilled. The day they would all return and they would all be as one united people. So, he asks for the same thing. Only he asks for it when they return as a people, to the land God gave them. This would come only when God said to leave.

Dear Lord Jesus,

You love us more than we can comprehend. You open our eyes to things around us, and things yet to come. Lord, Your blessings are not always in what we can see and touch, but much deeper in that they reach our very souls. Your sacrifice in the place of our due payment for our sins is greater and far weightier than anything I could have ever expected. You did for us something we could never do for ourselves. Lord, help me to live this example You set, by daily immersing myself in Your Word.

In Jesus name, Amen.

BIBLIOGRAPHY

Hassett, B., & Sağlamtimur, H. (2018, June 27). Radical 'royals'? Burial practices at Başur Höyük and the emergence of early states in Mesopotamia. *Antiquity*, 640 – 654. Retrieved from https://www.cambridge.org/core/journals/antiquity/article/abs/radical-royals-burial-practices-at-basur-hoyuk-and-the-emergence-of-early-states-in-mesopotamia/23E69D907B072E3789D-C5B4F72108AC6

www.ingramcontent.com/pod-product-compliance
Lightning Source LLC
LaVergne TN
LVHW010226070526
838199LV00062B/4746